A TRIP TO THE PRAIRIES

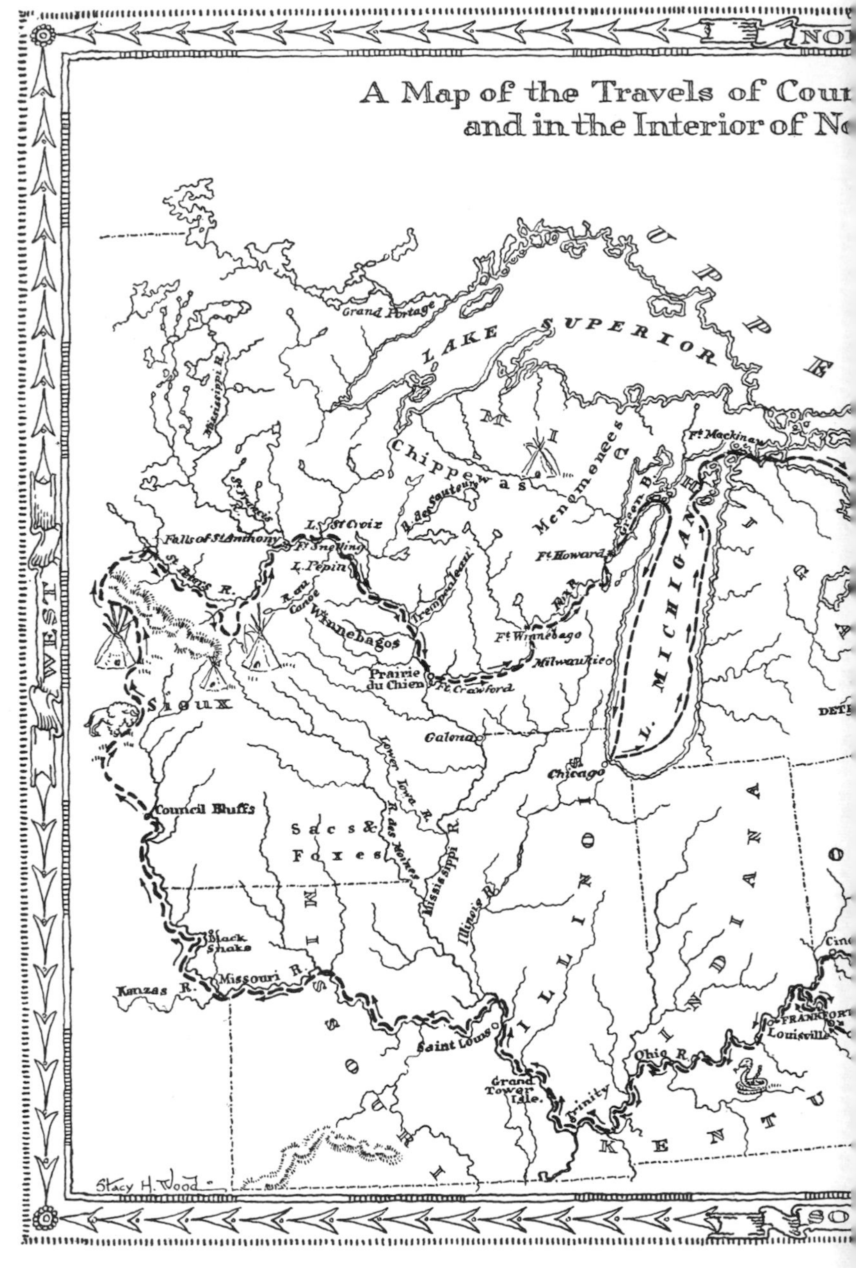

A Map of the Travels of Cou
and in the Interior of N
NO
WEST
SO
LAKE SUPERIOR
UPPER
Grand Portage
Mississippi R.
Chippewas
Menomenees
Ft Mackinaw
Green B.
L. MICHIGAN
Falls of St Anthony
L. St Croix
Ft Snelling
L. Pepin
St Peters R.
Winnebagos
Prairie du Chien
Ft Crawford
Ft Howard
Ft Winnebago
Milwaukie
Sioux
Galena
Chicago
Council Bluffs
Sacs & Foxes
Lower Iowa R.
R. des Moines
Mississippi R.
Illinois R.
ILLINOIS
INDIANA
Black Snake
Missouri R.
Kanzas R.
Saint Louis
Grand Tower Isle.
Ohio R.
Louisville
FRANKFORT
KENTU
Stacy H. Wood

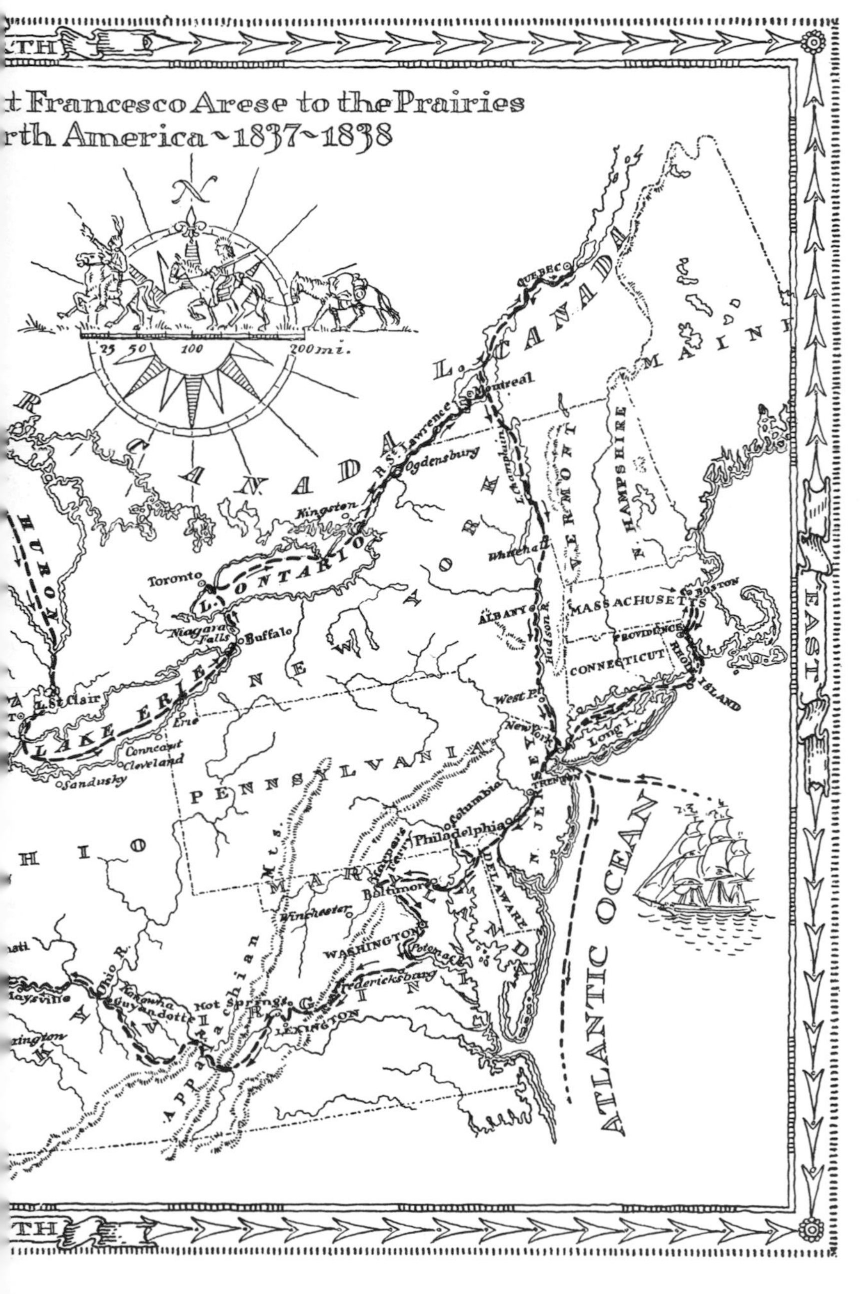
t Francesco Arese to the Prairies
rth America ~ 1837 ~ 1838
N
25 50 100 200 mi.
CANADA
L. CANADA
QUEBEC
Montreal
MAINE
N. HAMPSHIRE
VERMONT
MASSACHUSETTS
BOSTON
PROVIDENCE
RHODE ISLAND
CONNECTICUT
Long I.
NEW YORK
Ogdensburg
Kingston
Whitehall
L. Champlain
ALBANY
Hudson R.
West Pt.
New York
L. ONTARIO
Toronto
Niagara Falls
Buffalo
LAKE ERIE
L. St Clair
Erie
Conneaut
Cleveland
Sandusky
HURON
PENNSYLVANIA
Columbia
Philadelphia
TRENTON
N. JERSEY
DELAWARE
MARYLAND
Baltimore
Winchester
WASHINGTON
Potomac R.
Fredericksburg
VIRGINIA
LEXINGTON
Hot Springs
Appalachian Mts.
Ohio R.
Kanawha
Guyandotte
Maysville
KY
OHIO
ATLANTIC OCEAN
EAST

A TRIP TO THE

PRAIRIES

AND IN THE INTERIOR OF NORTH AMERICA [1837-1838]

Travel Notes

BY COUNT FRANCESCO ARESE

NOW FIRST TRANSLATED

FROM THE ORIGINAL FRENCH

By ANDREW EVANS

NEW YORK

COOPER SQUARE PUBLISHERS, INC.

1975

Originally Published 1934
Published 1975 by Cooper Square Publishers, Inc.
59 Fourth Avenue, New York, N. Y. 10003

Printed in the United States of America

Library of Congress Cataloging in Publication Data

Arese, Francesco, conte, 1805-1881.
A trip to the prairies and in the interior of North America, 1837-1838.
Reprint of the ed. published by Harbor Press, New York.
1. United States—Description and travel—1783-1848. I. Title.
E165.A63 1975 917.7'04'2 74-12556
ISBN 0-8154-0496-4

Printed in U.S.A. by
NOBLE OFFSET PRINTERS, INC.
New York, N.Y. 10003

Contents

Preface

ON THE TEXT

WHOEVER has travelled in the immense realm of Tolstoy's "War and Peace," will remember that the Russian characters speak in French as often as in their own language; the original is not entirely Russian. Similarly many of the leading characters in the intricate drama of the Risorgimento were at home in two languages, and a book like Bonfadini's "Arese," for instance, contains so much French correspondence between Italians, that its pages sometimes take on a curious look. The bilingual habit seems natural enough in the Piedmontese, who having a dialect for mother-tongue, learn in infancy to communicate with their neighbors on both sides; but one does wonder why Ricasoli a Tuscan and Arese a Lombard, should have written to each other in French. Such wondering makes us wonder less that Arese kept the journal of his American travels in French. Despite his ease, his was not quite the French of Paris: that very ease itself apparently led him to write some French words in an Italian way, and once at least, even to invent a word. If he did invent it, he no doubt did so unconsciously.

I say "apparently" and "if" because of the state of his Notes of "A Trip to the Prairies," as it comes to us printed in the last pages of the book containing his life ("Vita di Francesco Arese." R. Bonfadini. Torino, Roma. 1894). Still we cannot blame much on the typesetters (who also set the many French letters already mentioned), except for the remarkable errors in American geographical and proper names, which, whether Indian, English, or French, appear to have bothered them—or rather not have bothered them—sufficiently. Though Arese was occasionally careless, as when he wrote New York by a slip for New Castle, he seems to have tried his best, and to have done fairly well, especially in names frequently repeated. But whoever is to blame, gross errors are too many and too regular for it to have been worth while in most cases to call attention to them. Where any detective work was required, I have explained in a note.

As is evident from one or two passages, Arese, doubtless finding it inconvenient to jot down his do-ings and observations day by day, now and then found time to bring his journal to date. It is partly for that reason that there are some curious mixtures of tenses in it. At times I have made free to straighten these out. Although I have not tried in any way to work his Notes up into a semblance of the book Arese seems to have contemplated, but have adhered scrupulously to the endeavor to make the same impression in English that he makes in his French, still I have qualified that adherence by a certain amount of license. Rough the notes are and rough they remain. But besides the straightening out of tenses, and venturing to cut up his interminable paragraphs and interminable sentences (so inordinately long at times that—as will happen with a hurried writer—they become ambiguous or vague. But even when the words are not clear the sense almost always is: in not more than two cases has it been necessary to guess), I have divided the narrative into chapters, which it seemed naturally to separate into, and for which I have supplied headings.

Moreover, keeping in mind the comparative richness of the two languages, I have slightly enlarged his vocabulary, a poor one even for French. I have excised a bit of his redundancy. I believe that enough of both poverty and redundancy remains for all purposes. His exuberant Italian punctuation I have restrained into the possible limits of decent English printing: for instance, where he dashed in three exclamation points together, I have allowed him one. His rather few italics and arbitrary capitalizings I generally retain. All of which has been done for the purpose of making the book inviting.

Later in life Arese edited his Notes—after the "Great Western" had crossed the Atlantic and after his friend Louis Napoleon had become Emperor and given a name to the sort of goatee he wore. But the editing can scarcely have been drastic.

In 1881, the year Arese died, and apparently very shortly after his death, at a Geographical Congress in Venice, Cesare Correnti made a mediocre speech to introduce the Travel Notes, which he then read aloud.

A. E.

Translator's Introduction

THE Count Francesco Arese, born 1805, was the only child of noble Milanese parents, of whom his mother at least was very rich. At the Court of Eugène Beauharnais, Napoleonic Viceroy in Milan, she had known Eugène's sister Hortense, later Queen of Holland: an acquaintance that was to have a great deal to do with her son's future.

When he was nine, the Empire fell and the Austrians returned to their former Italian possessions. Two years later they arrested his uncle, they arrested family friends, who had been conspiring against them. The young Count grew up in a rebellious country, and like many young men of his time he was a rebel at heart, and even somewhat more.

When about twenty, while travelling with his mother, he met in Rome her old friend Hortense, with whose younger son, Louis Napoleon, he became very intimate.

In 1831 Louis Napoleon and his elder brother were prominent in an uprising in Romagna, which tried to free itself from Papal dominion, and which Austria helped hold in subjection. Hortense, extremely frightened about her sons, was not afraid to go into the midst of turmoil to rescue them. They caught measles, and the older one died. By means of ruses and stratagems worthy of any novel (and well recounted by her in her Memoirs), she managed to spirit the future Emperor away to England.

Arese was, of course, in full sympathy with his friend. At about this time he himself was deep in conspiracies; so much so that he was among a number of men about to be arrested. He was one of those that succeeded in getting out of the country. Thereon his mother wrote to Hortense, who had a castle called Arenenberg in the Canton of Turgovia, Switzerland, begging her to harbor the exile. Hortense had by then returned from England, and she answered very cordially, saying, " . . . my son will be delighted to have so good a hunting companion."

With the Bonapartes Arese spent over a year, mostly at Arenenberg, but partly in trips with his friend, even so far as to London. Both were rather serious, studious young men, interested in practical activities, and above all in what was for both of them the most practical of all activities, politics.

Arese's mother considered other things more important: for instance, a good marriage for her son. In 1832 Hortense's husband (who lived in Florence, apart from his wife) suggested a wealthy French girl; but the girl's mother would not run the risk of her daughter's living in foreign parts. Then Louis proposed a cousin of his wife's, niece to the Queen of Sweden. Arese, meanwhile, had chosen a girl for himself. His mother was so opposed to his choice that he abandoned it; not, apparently, with any deep regret, but with considerable discontent at his mother's domineering ways. He was proud. When he learned that his mother had obtained for him from the Austrian court, on condition that he ask for it himself, permission to return home, he was much upset. Then his mother cut off, or stringently reduced, his monthly allowance. Upon that, Arese took advantage of a visit made at Arenenberg by a son of the French marshal Clauzel. Furnished with a recommendation, he hastened to Algeria which the French were conquering, and enrolled as a cavalryman in the newly-founded Foreign Legion. Later he became an officer and was on Clauzel's staff. He remained in Africa two years.

Meanwhile his friends remonstrated with his

mother. Queen Hortense joined her efforts to the others, writing affectionately of the young man. Finally the mother yielded on all points, restored her son's allowance to its former figure, and even offered an extra amount for emergencies; of which Arese, despite all his travels, never availed himself.

Before leaving Africa, he made a trip to see the country and study the natives, going as far inland as the Sahara. On his return to Europe, his first visit was to Arenenberg.

A few months later, in the Fall of 1836, an attempt at a Bonapartist restoration was made at Strasbourg. It failed totally, and Louis Napoleon was taken prisoner. The government of Louis Philippe, through either generosity or caution, preferred exile for the Prince, and shipped him on a naval vessel to America. On hearing this, Arese hurried to Arenenberg and offered to go to New York to be with the Prince. Hortense, besides being a devoted mother with her devotion centred on the one remaining son of three, was now also a sick woman, and accepted his offer with joy. He hastened to Liverpool and sailed—literally, for the time of transatlantic steamers had not quite arrived.

His crossing took fifty days; but even then he was

in New York before his comrade. As he wrote to a friend: "I have been in terrible anxiety, because not only had Louis not arrived here, but there was not even news of him or his frigate. But finally yesterday a vessel brought the news that the frigate with Louis aboard was at Rio Janeiro and about to sail for this port." He did not guess that the captain had had sealed orders to go to Hampton Roads (where, according to the "New York Spectator," the Prince landed) via Brazil.

After the death of the Emperor Francis I a few months before, a number of Italian prisoners had been released from the Spielberg and had betaken themselves to New York, probably as a good place for conspiring. With them Arese and the Prince, who was as eager as anybody to free Italy, spent some of their time. The Prince's uncle Joseph, who lived at Bordentown, New Jersey, had gone to Europe the Summer before; and anyway he was cross with his nephew about Strasbourg. The busy Philip Hone, although he mentions Joseph with condescending approval in his "Diary" (New York, 1927), did not like Bonapartes and did not meet Louis. He noted his departure on 12 June, "after walking Broadway during the last three or four weeks." Arese tells us that he himself left New York on 11 June. It seems strange that after coming so far to be with his friend he should not wait one day to see him sail. But we know that Hone was given to copying bits from newspapers, and a glance at "The New York Spectator" explains the difficulty. In its bi-weekly number of 12 June it announces that the Prince has taken passage on the "George Washington," and in the advertisement of the Liverpool Packets in the same number we find that the monthly sailing to England was by the "George Washington" on the 8th. Neither announcements nor ads were very up-to-date in 1837. From Arese's writing of being "well received in Society and much entertained," as well as from his having letters to such people as Henry Clay and the Chouteaus, we may conclude that the young men were not always walking Broadway. Besides, the Prince told Henry Wikoff who called on him at Ham ("Napoleon Louis Bonaparte," New York, 1847, chap. VIII) about the attention paid him in America. New York Society was hardly so different then that a real Count and an Imperial Prince would have been neglected.

In certain other details Hone bears Arese out strikingly:—as to "No matter" and "Go ahead," the burning of the "Ben Sherrod," and the frequent falling down of scarcely completed buildings; to note a few.

His friend gone, Arese was again seized with the desire to see strange men and modes of life; perhaps that is why he did not return to Europe with him. Louis had rushed homeward on receipt of the following letter:

"My dear Son!

"It is absolutely necessary for me to have an operation; if it should not be successful, I send you my blessing in this letter.

"We shall meet again, shall we not, in a better world where you are not to come and join me until as late as possible! and you will remember that I leave this one with no regret except for you, for your sweet affection which is the only thing that made me find some charm here. It will be a consolation for you, my dear friend, to think that by your attentions you have made your mother happy, as much so as she could be; you will think of all my fondness for you, and you will have courage!

"Believe that one looks down tenderly and clearly on what one has left here below; for surely we shall meet again; cling to that lovely idea, it is too necessary not to be true.

"That nice Arese, I give him my blessing too, as to a son.—I press you to my heart, my dear.

"I am quite calm, quite resigned, and I am still in hopes that we shall meet once more in this world.—God's will be done!

Your devoted mother,

"3 April, 1837. "HORTENSE."

In those days, before anesthetics, an operation was a terrific ordeal.

Arese left New York, headed in a different direction; and during the ensuing months, he wrote in his diary the Notes herewith published. He was then 32. Part of his trip, between Council Bluffs and Fort Snelling, if not further, was still pretty wild travelling. The authors of "Minnesota in Three Centuries" judge that "in all, not fifty white men had passed over the tract of country now comprising Southern and Southwestern Minnesota . . . in 1849." Arese did it twelve years before that, at the period when Nicollet did not consider his party of nineteen men, one of them an army officer, quite enough for complete safety in very nearly the same region where Arese, with two companions, roved so gaily, though not indeed foolhardily.

In October Hortense died, without having had the operation. In her will she left Arese a large carved turquoise. When he some months later returned to Europe, the Prince at once invited him to Arenenberg, but Arese, for what reason we do not know, refused. He divided his time between London and Paris, until in September 1838 the new Austrian régime permitted Italian exiles to go home. Arese as well as the rest, went; and for the next few years he lived in Milan. The new Austrian government was milder than the previous one, and possibly for that reason the methods of the revolutionists were milder. Instead of secret societies and armed revolts, they went in for technical schools and magazines, and by example won over Society to eschew balls at the Viceregal court.

Arese married: his mother died and left him her large fortune. For three years after America he did not see Louis; and then for some years he had no chance to. In the early forties Louis wrote asking him to join a party, along with the Count of Wurtemberg (Louis's first cousin by marriage) and others, for a trip in Greece. Arese did not wish to leave his young family; and Louis was prevented from going. The Bonapartist demonstration at Boulogne, this time landed him in prison at Ham. With him went his fellow-conspirator, doctor, and lifelong friend Conneau; who to judge by his letters, was also a devoted friend of Arese's, with as ardent a desire for the liberation of Italy as the Prince, as (we might almost say) Arese himself. A good many letters passed between Milan and Ham; and Arese seems to have furnished books and apparatus for the endless studies and experiments the prisoners pursued.

At last '48 came, a year of revolution. There was a famous uprising in Milan; but Arese who wanted his part in the fighting, was sent to Turin to see whether the King of Sardinia would join the Lombard patriots against Austria. Unable to swim, unable to procure a boat, Arese had to let a peasant carry him across the river-frontier, which must have recalled incidents in America. The King was friendly. A couple of days later Arese was in the field. While his company was being inspected by the general, a grenade fell nearby and burst. Almost everybody dropped to the ground for safety, but not Arese. When the general asked him why, he said, "I was waiting for my superior officer to set me the example."

The revolutionists being short of cannon, he bought them some. He was sent as one of the ambassadors to Bavaria, where Hortense's sister-in-law Amalia Beauharnais was an influential personage. Despite that, Bavaria would not recognize the new government. Despite everything, the new government fell. Arese retired to Genoa, in the Kingdom of Sardinia.

On the whole no great material advance came in that year to the cause of Italian independence. But in December, in France where revolution had been more successful, Louis Napoleon was elected President of the Second Republic. Gioberti, the Sardinian premier, sent Arese to Paris to congratulate the new ruler in the name of King Charles Albert. He was received most cordially by the comrade he had taken leave of in New York almost twelve years before.

From then on the story of the two is more and more a part of European history. Arese lost his wife, he became a Sardinian subject, refused to stand for election as a Deputy and was accordingly made Senator by the King. In 1851 he went to London to see the first of all Universal Exhibitions. On the way home he stopped to visit his old friend again; and when a few months later that old friend became Emperor, Arese was prompt to write him. The Emperor was equally prompt in replying to *"un ami comme vous."*

The next year he went twice to Paris: once Napoleon put him up at the Tuileries, and made him the bearer of a message to the new King Victor Emanuel II—an invitation to Paris.

Arese made it a principle to take no part in purely French politics. If he had private opinions as to anything his old comrade did, he kept them private. Most likely that very discretion was one strong reason for their continued friendship. Possibly that was the reason why Arese was the only Italian, as Dr.

Conneau wrote him more than once, whom Eugénie could abide. One time he wrote: "You are omnipotent here: you can say and do to the Empress what nobody else could permit himself to do and say."

But Italian politics was Arese's life, and in questions about the relations of his own country to her great neighbor he did not feel much hesitation. When in 1852 the French minister at Turin had made himself unpopular, Arese was the person to write direct to the Emperor about it. An "inspired" letter from Conneau was the answer; and with the proper diplomatic delay and gentleness the offensive agent was withdrawn.

In 1855 during the Crimean War, Arese was again invited to Paris: there and at St. Cloud he lived with the imperial couple and shared their meals. He wrote afterwards, "You have both treated me like one of the family."

Throughout all this time, whenever there was a letter to be written to the Emperor in view of the aid Italian patriots expected he was some day going to give them against Austria, almost invariably Arese was called upon to write it. While Cavour, representing Sardinia at the Congress of Paris after the Crimean War, was doing marvels to bring that small country into prominence, he constantly wrote Arese about what was going on, especially behind the scenes. Once he thanks him for having arranged, in Conneau, a means of direct personal access to the Emperor.

Finally in '59 the chance came and Napoleon III took an army into Italy to aid Victor Emanuel against the Austrians. The King appointed Arese one of two special envoys to welcome "the August ally." Eugénie wrote Arese, "I am trying, *as hard as I can,* to become Italian."

The war was very short, because as soon as the Emperor thought the Italians had gained enough, he unexpectedly withdrew. The Italians did not feel that they had gained enough. However, some of them were grateful, and all were officially grateful. Still Cavour at once resigned, and Arese was called to form a ministry. He found himself, after a trial, unable to do so.

He did, a little later, go again to Paris and again was the personal guest of the Emperor, whom he endeavored to persuade to his view of what France might yet do for Italy. He was scarcely home before he was sent back on the same errand. In the intricate negotiations that went on under the surface of formal diplomacy, with a view to remaking the map of Italy, Arese appears to have been the individual whose honesty, tact, and power of accomplishment everybody trusted in, both as to Italy and as to the relations between Italy and France. In the extremely delicate question of transferring Savoy and Nice to the French Empire, as payment for participation in the war, Arese continued to serve Cavour (now again premier) as "a spur, a buffer, and a lightning-rod for his friend the Emperor."

At last things were settled and the Kingdom of Italy began: an Italy still lacking Venice and Rome. When Arese, although in bad health, was chosen to carry to Napoleon III the letter in which Victor Emanuel announced his new title, it was largely because of the opportunity thus given for confidential talk with the Emperor about the prospects of adding Rome to the new realm. Cavour had suddenly died; but Ricasoli, now prime minister, was glad to continue using the buffer and lightning-rod.

It was another ten years before the Kingdom was rounded out to the dimensions it retained up to the end of the World War; during which the friendship between Arese and his old crony did not lapse. In '64 Napoleon wrote congratulating him on his daughter's marriage. In '66, at the time of Italy's disastrous interference in the war Prussia made on Austria, Arese once again went to Paris to see what could be cooked up with the Emperor. What was cooked up, but by the Emperor without Arese's knowledge, did not please the Italians, though it gave them Venice at last. Even then Lamarmora got Arese to write to Conneau: and finally he wrote to the Emperor to see what could be done about Rome. The Emperor's answer was unsatisfactory.

Arese appears to have been a trifle piqued. At any rate, when he went to the Paris Exposition of '67 he didn't call on his old companion. He made a plausible excuse, however, and two years later did go to visit the imperial family at Compiègne. That was the last time he saw Louis Napoleon.

He received a letter from him in 1869, a very friendly letter; and the year after that Louis was an exile in England and Arese, with all his old friendliness, tact, and scrupulous honesty, was helping him sell some imperial property in Rome to the Italian government, now finally in possession there. In this negotiation Victor Emanuel addresses Arese as "dearest Count and Cousin," for he had shortly before bestowed on him the "Grand Collar of the Annunciation," and that entitled him to such treatment.

In 1873 Napoleon III died. Eugénie continued to correspond affectionately with Arese. From a couple of articles by Carlo Pagani ("Napoleone III Eugenia di Montijo e Francesco Arese in un Carteggio Inedito," in the "Nuova Antologia," 1-16 Gennaio, 1921) we learn that Eugénie wrote to "his" (the Emperor's) "best friend," to wish he were with her in her grief; to ask his advice about a letter she planned writing to Victor Emanuel; to say that her son, departing for Zululand, had left a good-bye for him; to bid him adieu before she "left Europe" (apparently to go to England). It has been suggested that they were in love. Most probably they were not. There appears to be slight foundation for such a charge except in her letters; and those, although deeply affectionate, are not love-letters.

During Arese's last illness she wrote to his son, offering to come to her old friend. He died in 1881, at the age of 76.

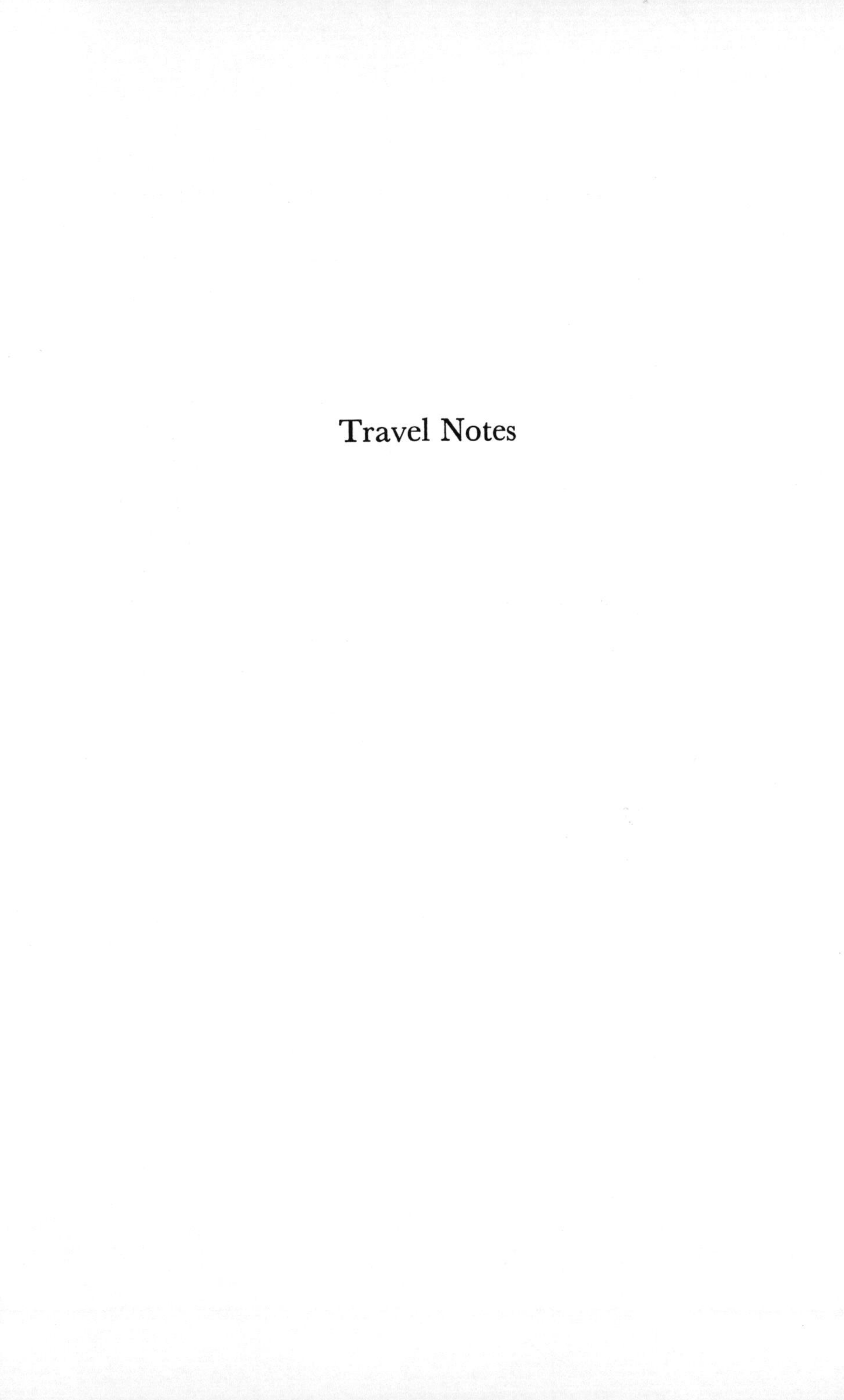

Travel Notes

Travel Notes

[I]

From New York, by Rail and Steamboat, via Philadelphia and Baltimore, to Washington.

ON the 11 June 1837, at 9 in the morning, I left New York for Philadelphia, where I arrived at 5 that afternoon, having made the trip partly by steamboat—first on an arm of the sea between Staten Island and New Jersey, then on the Delaware—and partly by rail. Before speaking of the country, I will say two words about the steamboats. Despite whatever pride I may have as a European, I must admit that we in Europe cannot form any idea of the size and the luxuriousness of American steamboats. The finest ones we have in Europe are much inferior to the smallest, the wretchedest ferry-boat over here, where, parenthetically, the ferries also run by steam. In all the boats there are gentlemen's saloons and a ladies' saloon, berths for two or three and various buildings. From Bordentown, where one takes another steamboat, to Philadelphia, both banks of the crooked Delaware are flat. Philadelphia, if not the most poetical town, is at least the prettiest, the best built, and the cleanest, that I ever saw. It is quite flat, the streets form right angles and are wide, straight, regular, and so clean that there is nothing to compare them to. In Philadelphia you see none of those ugly barracks, sort of huge sentry-boxes, that mar Broadway, New York's best street; nor do you see, as in the latter city, a discordant incongruousness of houses that puts your eyes out. Here the houses are of brick with white marble ornamentation; there are even seen buildings entirely of white marble, the most striking of which are the Girard Exchange,* the United States Bank, and various churches and theatres, which decorate the city elegantly, and can be criticized only for a certain lack of taste in their architecture, a fault one finds nearly everywhere in America, where the feeling for art and for beauty is as yet unknown. One of the most attractive things in Philadelphia is the market; everything is so clean, so elegant, so tastefully arranged, that you almost feel you are seeing

*It seems probable that Arese confused the Exchange with Girard College and perhaps made one building out of two.

a panorama or a theatrical performance. The Philadelphians are very proud of their water-works, and have reason to be. Those works consist of a simple machine that pumps the water from the Schuylkill up to the top of a hill where it is received in four large reservoirs, which distribute it to the entire town. On this hill they have made a charming promenade from which there is a lovely view of the Schuylkill and its picturesque banks.

The railway to Columbia is worthy of mention because of a large engine designed to haul the cars up and let them down on a part of the line that has a grade of 10%. I happened to notice that the big cable working the motor was made of Italian hemp from Bologna. I could not say for what reason, but I found that rope magnificent, the most interesting part of the apparatus. I wanted to examine the inside of the machine in detail, but its owner guarded it jealously from intruders. On my way back from Belmont* I saw the famous garden of Mr. Pratt,† which has noth-

* Belmont on the Schuylkill is now well within the city of Philadelphia.

† According to Walter Rendell Storey in the "New York Times Magazine," May 10, 1931, pp. 16, 17, this was "Lemon Hill, built in 1798 on the site of Robert Morris's country estate, where in his famous greenhouse he grew the first lemon trees

ing remarkable about it except its fine position close to the Schuylkill.

I visited the two penitentiaries. Outside they are Gothic in style and look like two great Mediæval castles. Inside they are very nicely built, of stone, and clean beyond comparison. The prisoners are better lodged, better fed than most of the pupils in the boarding-schools of a large portion of Europe; and I might even venture to say that they are almost too comfortable. Each one has a room of his own, and in one of these prisons the men have, besides, each a little yard to exercise in; but the women have instead, a second room. All the prisoners have beds with mattresses, and clean sheets every week, the requisites for working at a trade, and in each room there is a water-faucet and a water-closet. It is a very sad thing for humanity to have to say that in spite of all this, and of all possible systems, any improvement in the character of the inmates is scarcely noticeable, or so the various directors of those institutions assured me. The commonest crime is larceny, and the ratio of blacks to white, in proportion to population, is very large.

that Philadelphia had ever seen. Morris sold the property to Henry Pratt. . . . The mansion is now occupied by Mr. and Mrs. Fiske Kimball."

One rather strange thing is that, though the prisoners have knives and iron instruments for use in their trades, they never attack their keepers, and suicide is quite unknown.

When I left these institutions, I wanted to show my gratitude to the porter, who had guided me through them, by giving him a small coin, but he refused absolutely to take it.* In America everything is paid for, nothing is given away. People do their duty, and nothing to oblige. The porter was paid by the institution.

The various things manufactured by the prisoners were excellently made. Any sums obtained by selling them, in one of the prisons, go entirely to the State, which keeps an account with the States the prisoners belong to. However, when a prisoner is released, he gets a suit of clothes and six écus.† In the other prison, the inmates when

* Robert James Turnbull, in his "Visit to the Philadelphia Prison," Philadelphia 1796, states that he also was surprised by the guide's refusing a tip. The "Pennsylvania System" was of so much interest in many places that a French translation of Turnbull's account was published in Paris in "l'an VIII" (1800).

† The écu varied very much in value at different times and in different places; it would seem probable that Arese meant six dollars. He was of course told in dollars, and would have no reason to convert the amount in his head, and some écus were worth very nearly a dollar.

set free get approximately half of what they have earned, the expense of their keep being deducted.

The Navy Yard or Arsenal would not deserve mention, were it not that the "Pennsylvania" was there, a man-of-war of 140 guns, an immense structure which, in a few days from now, will be afloat. She will be launched the 18 or 20 July. She has 3 decks and 1/2, is 227 feet long by 60 wide; the height of her mainmast above water level is 130 feet; her tonnage is 3000. 1200 men are required to run her. When completed and armed, she will have cost $500,000; and it will cost the State $400,000 a year to keep her, in war-time. This ship, which will cost twice as much as two frigates of the first class, will be less useful, for in time of war she will be good only for coastwise service, to prevent blockades. To show her off they are going to send her to make a parade-tour in Europe, and after that will use her as a school-ship. I hope I may be permitted to say that in this country, which furnishes the best sailors, the sturdiest and bravest sailors in the world, there is no naval academy, and everything goes rather by chance, and with excellent results. It appears that the Americans being, as they maintain, very religious, have not wished to leave Providence nothing to do, and so have given it special charge of their ships and steamers, which, if Providence naps or forgets, sink, burn, or blow up.

I have spent a day in the country to see the environs, which are charming, especially the banks of the Schuylkill. I visited various points where there was a view worthy of admiration. In several villages I noticed manufactories, mostly of cotton.

The hotels here are not so big as those in New York, but on the other hand the service is far better. In several stores I went into, I observed a politeness and courtesy that one would hunt for in vain in the New York shops. I have been forgetting one little observation, a very little one, but one that seems to me an excellent illustration of the American character: at the larger of the two prisons there is a rather high tower with a lightning-rod on it; only they have forgotten to run it into the ground, so that the object of this lightning-rod is to attract lightning to the tower instead of allowing it to strike one of the trees in the surrounding fields, should it so prefer. In America, so long as things have been made and above all quickly made, whether badly or well is of slight importance. In New York I saw houses built in a very few days, but they were falling to pieces before the roofs were on. If some men were killed—"No matter!",* a very common phrase in America.

I have also been through the National Museum, which gives an exact idea of the birth of the arts and the sciences—a few dozen pebbles, some wretched portraits of men worthy of much better fame, some miserable animals not quite badly enough stuffed to make the rats and moths respect them, an old Arab saddle,† Indian costumes, a Mexican sabre, and a French helmet picked up on the field of Waterloo and ornamented with a large inscription. I did not bother my head much about the Mexican sabre, but as for the French helmet, I wondered why it was there. Was it in order to have a share in the glory that only chance and treason procured for their former compatriots, or was it to show gratitude to the French for the help they gave them during their war of independence? On my oath, I can't figure it out, and I don't believe the Americans can either. All in all, their museum would not be out of place on the quay in Paris where old iron is sold.

Unfortunately I have not much I can say about Society in Philadelphia; but the few people I

* In English in the text.

† The text has "salle," which surely is a misprint for "selle."

have met, especially ladies, have certainly given me an exalted idea of their hospitality and amiability. I left Philadelphia for Baltimore on board one of the usual magnificent steamboats: on the Delaware to New Castle,* then by railroad to French Town, and from there in another steamboat on the Elk River and Chesapeake Bay to Baltimore. The region I travelled through offers nothing very remarkable excepting Chesapeake Bay, which is so enormously wide that it would not be difficult to believe oneself on the ocean.

Coming up to Baltimore you see Fort McHenry,† but the weather was not clear enough for me to see it very well. After Philadelphia, Baltimore did not make an extremely agreeable impression on me. The streets are not handsome, and they are so empty that you could use them for a rifle-range without fear of wounding any one. The most noteworthy things are the monuments.

* The text says "New York," undoubtedly a slip of Arese's pen. The delightful "Illustrated Atlas, Geographical, Statistical, and Historical, of the United States, and the Adjacent Countries" by T(homas) G(amaliel) Bradford, Boston, n.d. (Copyrighted, 1838) shows clearly that the railway ran from New Castle, Delaware.

† The original says "le fort Fleury." This time I think that Arese omitted the "Mc" and that the rest was a misprint. In handwriting Fl may often be easily mistaken for an H, and of course small u and small n are alike in the average handwriting.

One of them, to Washington, is a tall column with a statue of the great man. This monument would be really beautiful, if the thickness of the pedestal did not spoil it. From the top there is rather a pretty, though not an extensive outlook. The other monument, neither large nor beautiful, was erected in memory of the citizens who died in 1814 fighting against the English, whom they repulsed.

In the evening I had the unhappy idea of going to the theatre. No, the liveliest and most daring imagination would be puzzled to form an idea of the Baltimore theatre! The darkness was very slightly broken by a few poor tallow candles; but one could not complain too much about that, because the shadows did something to hide the dirtiness of the theatre and of the audience, who, to tell the truth, were of the lowest class. The programme comprised "The Tower of Notre Dame," and the "Capture of Algiers." In the third act there was a "Court of Miracles," which was such a miracle of absurdity that I began to laugh hysterically. Fearing the hisses might lead to other more concrete and violent demonstrations, I thought it prudent to decamp. I consoled myself for not seeing Algiers by the sweet reflection that the Algiers I had really seen would leave me a more exact and charming souvenir than any I could have got from the Algiers of the Baltimore theatre. In New York admission costs $1, at Philadelphia 3/4, and at Baltimore 1/2. Taking everything into consideration, Baltimore is, in its atmosphere, much more the small town than Philadelphia, and very much more than New York. I met very few people there, but those I did meet I found most amiable and hospitable. They were good enough to give me all possible information about that region.

From Baltimore I went to Harper's Ferry by railway. The country is rather fine. The line runs along the Patapsco, and there are pretty farms on the banks, and a fertile, well-cultivated soil. At about 50 miles from Baltimore we reached Point of Rocks, where the Potomac first becomes visible. The Shenandoah has already flowed into it at Harper's Ferry. The view is magnificent, varied by the crookedness of the river and by several fine rocks, and above all by the Blue Ridge, which can be seen far away. The outskirts of Harper's Ferry are sublimely beautiful. To reach the town you go over a bridge 900 feet long, which crosses both rivers at their junction. I climbed to the top of a hill called Jefferson's Rock, above Harper's Ferry. It is one of the most beautiful outlooks imaginable. In order to give a good description, I will quote what Jefferson himself said:

"The passage of the Potomac through the Blue "Ridge is, perhaps, one of the most stupendous "scenes in nature. You stand on a very high point "of land; on your right comes down the Shenan-"doah, having ranged along the foot of the moun-"tain an hundred miles, to seek a vent. On your "left approaches the Potomac, in quest of a pas-"sage also; in the moment of their junction, they "rush together against the mountain, rend it "asunder and pass on to the sea." *

Near the top of the hill are a Catholic church and a Masonic Hall. The rock has been given the name of Jefferson because it is from there that he wrote his description, and he could certainly not have chosen a better place, for the view one enjoys from there is such as to electrify the soul, even a soul of ice. The railroad from Baltimore to Harper's Ferry is the one called the "Baltimore and Ohio," which at present goes only to Winchester, that is to say covers only a few miles, but which will soon be extended as far as Wheeling.

This railway is a very good example of the enterprising courage of the Americans; and Europeans in general, and Italians in particular, ought

* In English in the text; and here corrected.

certainly to wish to exchange (if that were possible) some of their paintings and statues for a few leagues of railway. I went to see a musket factory belonging to the State, which turns out 12,000 a year, and a carbine factory, which turns out 9,000. The carbines are breech-loading and not rifled, but their barrels diminish toward the muzzle, and instead of a ramrod they have a bayonet so long and thin that it did not appear strong enough to pierce a belt-strap and gave rather more the impression of a spit than of a bayonet.

I left Harper's Ferry for Washington by the canal. The boat, though not big, was very nice-looking and comfortable, and had two saloons, one for ladies and one for men. I dined and lunched on board very well: for instance, they gave us ice-water, a comfort not to be exaggerated, and one found everywhere in America, even in hamlets consisting only of a stable for the stage-horses and a log-house for the hostlers—a place where you stop just to change horses, and where you can have all the ice you want without there ever being a question of paying anything for it. The boat is towed by two horses, changed every hour, and she makes six miles an hour. The country is lovely, and the two aqueducts, Monocacy and the one called Seneca, are magnificent. Near

Seneca I saw the town of Berlin, consisting of three wooden houses. Although American towns are printed in large letters on the map, they are generally microscopic on the ground.

I also saw a place where there is a quarry of a marble called Pudding-Stone because of its resemblance to that dish. With that stone they have built the Capitol at Washington. I saw the waterfalls of the Potomac, which are inferior to those at Schaffhausen. The canal follows the course of the Potomac, and therefore there is always a fine view. Washington, except for the President's house and the Capitol, might be called a disappointment. One might strive in vain to find a city there. All there is are one big street and some houses scattered here and there. But happily for the Americans, it would be a huge mistake to judge the United States by its capital. The Capitol is an immense building, whose principal parts consist of a great rotunda with a dome, the Chamber of Commons (*sic*) (which is not so fine as the one in Paris, or perhaps even the one in Brussels) and the Senate Chamber. The rest of the structure is occupied by a library and offices. As usual, there are a great many columns, good statues in Carrara marble, and a monument to the brave sailors who lost their lives at Tripoli. In the rotunda there are paintings, which I was assured are fine. Unfortunately I could not judge for myself, because the dome was being restored and on that account the pictures were covered. On the whole, the Capitol is a big and fairly handsome building, well placed on an eminence. The President's residence makes a pretty good impression. I saw his reception rooms, which are excellently furnished. On one white marble console I noticed a German papier-maché snuff-box with the President's portrait. The house is in the middle of a garden, which is raised about three feet above the surrounding ground and not separated by either walls or fences, ditches, or hedges. And apropos of that, I think it needless to say that the guard-house and the sentry-boxes have been entirely forgotten. All you do is knock at the door; a white or a black servant tells you, without any master of ceremonies, grand chamberlain, grand esquire, or other anthropophagos being required, whether or not the President is at home. In the latter case, he tells you, "The President holds a public reception between 10 and noon." The next day, if you feel inclined, it is sufficient to hand in your card and you can have the honor of being presented.

The offices of the various ministries are in buildings of a uniform appearance not far from the President's house. I forgot to say that the Capitol rotunda is 96 feet in diameter and in height, that it is adorned with a handsome bronze statute of Jefferson, cast in Paris, and that the marble statues decorating the façade are by an Italian artist.

From Washington I went to Alexandria, a very pretty little town. From there I went on to Mount Vernon, which was George Washington's last residence after he relinquished the Presidency. His tomb is there. It was Sunday, and the lady of the house, widow of a nephew of the celebrated General* does not allow visitors on her property that day. I wrote her a note, and she was not only so kind as to make an exception in my case because I am a foreigner, but also so polite as to have refreshments served to me, fruit and wines. I infinitely regretted not being able to thank her in person for being extremely obliging. The house is prettily built and well placed, on a hill whence one enjoys a beautiful view over the Potomac. The garden and the park are everything that could be desired. Inside the house one sees the General's spy-glass, two chairs and a marble

* Jane Charlotte Washington (née Blackburn) was the widow of John Augustine, a grand-nephew of Washington's.

mantel-piece sent to Washington by Lafayette, and the keys of the Bastille in Paris. In the park there is a sort of little room or chapel built of red brick with a small iron door, above which the following words from Holy Scripture are chiselled: "I am the resurrection and the life: he that be- "lieveth in me, though he were dead, yet shall he "live, and whosoever liveth and believeth shall "never die.

"St. John, chap. xi, 25, 26."*

A few cedars and other trees spread their shade over this big dais or little room, and the whole is enclosed by a wall, and above the iron grill forming a fence, one reads:

Within this enclosure
Rest
The remains of General George Washington.†

The simplicity of the inscription and of the monument is entirely suitable to the simplicity of manner and character in that brave and upright citizen. Every man with a heart will understand better than I could express, the almost religious emotion I felt on finding myself, so to speak, on that holy ground. Despite the sign in

* In English in the text, but printed with some slight errors.
† In English in the text.

large letters forbidding any one to touch the trees and flowers that cover the tomb, I, with my guide's permission, plucked several small branches and some blossoms, for myself and for those of my friends who will know how to value them. The amount of land in the lady's property is 12,000 acres.

[11]

Across Virginia by Stage.

I RETURNED to Alexandria and to Washington, where I sailed on a Potomac steamboat to Potomac Creek,* whence I continued on by stagecoach to Fredericksburg, Orange Courthouse, and Charlottesville. I found nothing remarkable along the whole route, except one fine view of the Blue Ridge. We went through *the Gold Country*† without my becoming any the richer.

From Charlottesville I went to visit Monticello, the former residence of Jefferson. The house is charming and built with much taste and intelligence; but as the President died poor, it

* Arese says "Potomac break." Unable to find that on any map of the period or later, my guess is that he asked somebody on board, "What is that?" at the time they were in sight of the mouth of Potomac Creek, which flowed into the river a few miles above where the boat did land to connect with the stage he took; and that when he wrote up his diary, that was what came to him, very likely in the form of "Potomac break."

† English in the text. Alexander Brown says of this part of Virginia ("Genesis of the United States," 1890, p. 583, footnote 2), "now known as the eastern gold belt of Virginia." Pyrite is found there.

was sold cheap, I don't know to whom, but certainly to some wretched ostrogoth who instead of taking care of it, is allowing it to fall ignominiously to pieces. Its situation and the view from it surpass any possible words. On one side extends what I should like to call a mountainous plain—to speak a little more exactly, a very broken plain covered with forest, beyond which the Buckingham Mountains are visible, 80 miles away. On the other side one sees, first University, the site of the university built by Jefferson, who by means of a telescope oversaw the work from his garden and kept track of its daily progress. Beyond, there is a series of mountains all hemmed in by the Blue Ridge, which is seen in all its splendor. In the garden, which is worthy of the house, there is a monument to Jefferson, consisting of a simple little obelisk that one might more correctly call a marker, with a very simple inscription giving Jefferson's name and the date of his birth. I went to University, which takes its name from the university I mentioned above, that of the State of Virginia. Though on a small scale, its buildings are commodious and in excellent taste. The system of liberty, which reigns everywhere in the United States, might, with much profit, be restrained in regard to education. Certainly the nation would be a great gainer. The courses in medicine and surgery, for example, are too short; and it even happens quite often that men practice those professions without having finished the course or taken a degree. I met a number of professors and spent a most agreeable evening with them. Among others, there was one Penci from Milan, fencing and gymnastic master. The college or university, a mile away from Charlottesville, was built by Jefferson in 1826. It now has 265 students whose annual expense is $25,000, while each student spends $300. The college belongs to the State. Between Charlottesville and Staunton I made a detour, leaving the stagecoach route to visit Weyer's Cave and the New Cave. The cave, or grotto, called Weyer's was discovered by him by chance while he was hunting a porcupine.

The entrance to the cave is through a very low and very inconvenient little hole. I spent 3 hours visiting it. The stalactites are magnificent and gigantic. I sadly reflected that if the gentlemen who have taken the trouble to tell us that the earth is only 5000 odd years old, had come to visit this cave, when they saw the immense stalactites and considered how slowly those grow, they would not have hesitated an instant to call our earth a few centuries older. I afterwards visited the New Cave, where the stalactites are not so fine, but the cave itself is more grandiose and sublime. From Staunton I went to see the Warm Springs and the Hot Springs. The country everywhere in Virginia is magnificent and very interesting, for it affords admirable views every moment, and from the mountain-tops they are all the finer because, the summits being saddle-shaped and never flat, you can look out over two valleys at once.

The Warm and the Hot Springs, excepting for the beauty of their situations, do not deserve a visit. They form an exception in Virginia where all the little inns are clean and good, for here the rooms are small and dirty, and in some of them there are two beds and whether you will or no you have to sleep in the same room or sometimes even in the same bed with whoever happens along. I believe that if they were in Europe and you sent a mangy dog there, the dog, though an animal so affectionate and devoted to its master, would rebel rather than take the cure. On the road between Warm and Hot Springs, which I did on foot, I had a tussle with a rattlesnake, the first one I ever saw outside a cage. I killed it with my walking-stick and took its rattles for a trophy. There were seven of them, which shows that it was 7 years old, for they are its birth certificate, and it surely is a funny idea to carry that on the end of your tail. One thing that shocked me a good deal at Warm Springs was to read in the regulations:

> White servant per week — 6 dollars
> Colored ditto and Horses — 4 dollars.*

Although conscious of being in a State where slavery still flourishes, my dignity as a man was sorely wounded at seeing my fellow man, whether white or black, put on the same level as an animal. I shall say nothing as to the usefulness of slavery or its abolition. So much has been talked about it that nothing new remains to be said. I shall limit myself to remarking that the negroes who are slaves are far more industrious, cleaner, happier, healthier than the free ones, and that they are not the object of the flat, absurd witticisms of the whites, as is unhappily the case in the States where slavery has been abolished. This is not because the dignity of man or the self-respect of those unfortunates is more respected in those where slavery still exists, for the slave is not considered as a man, but as money; and money is much more respected

* In English in the text.

than self-respect is or the dignity of man or anything else besides money.

The Warm Springs' water is sulphureous and has a temperature of 98° Fahrenheit; the Hot Springs are also sulphureous and from 98° to 106. I went from Hot Springs to see the Natural Bridge and was obliged to spend a day on the way: it was the 4th of July and I was enchanted to see that national holiday. The evening before there was a great display of fireworks; 5 rockets were sent up, and 3 of them were star-rockets of 5 stars apiece, and not very bright stars at that. As for the other two, it would be hard for me to describe them, since one of them wouldn't go off and the other one, instead of shooting into the air, thought it better to burrow into the ground. The next morning the musket-firing began and the band of the volunteers or National Guard played national anthems in the street, and pretty well too. The review was at 8, and the men, without having too martial an air, were well set-up. Their uniforms were passably clean, but had the fault of all the American uniforms I have seen, that of being too richly embroidered and too theatrical. At 11 everybody went to the church where the minister read the Declaration of Independence, and followed it with an excellent politico-moral sermon.

Then the band played the national airs of "Hail, Columbia" and "Yankee Doodle," and then the crowd dispersed, to meet again at 3 for dinner. They did me the honor to admit me to a banquet that might truly be called political and patriotic, and I was greatly flattered. There were 160 odd people there, and though Americans are accused of being not too sober, I am forced to say that not a soul got drunk. After the dinner, which didn't last over ½ hour, several toasts were drunk. The first was to "the 4th of July, 1776," the next to General George Washington, the third to General Lafayette; and many others followed. Among the banqueters were two old veterans that had served under Washington, one of whom was a negro who had gone everywhere with the brave general, and for that reason, a half-century later, he was allowed the honor once every year of sitting down to table with white men! There was nothing, absolutely nothing in this celebration that suggested in the remotest degree that trumped-up joy, that official gaiety they gratify us with in Europe, quite contrary to our desire. Here the joy, the enthusiasm, were real, natural, heartfelt. Everything was authentic. Each individual was rightly proud to feel himself an American. Each one believed himself to share the glory of Washington, Jefferson, Marshall, and the other illustrious men whom not only America but the whole world, has the right to be proud of. Oh, God, when shall my own beautiful and wretched country be able to celebrate a day like that? It was regretfully that I the next day quitted the dear little town where I had experienced so many emotions, sweet and sad at the same time, but all very lively, to go see the Natural Bridge. This bridge, called "Natural" because Nature made it, might perhaps with even better reason be called the supernatural bridge, so large is it and so sublime in its savage beauty. The bridge is 240 and more feet above the little brook called Cedar Creek. The length of the arc is 60 feet and its thickness 45. Magnificent as it really is, I am not certain it would make the same effect if placed over the Via Mala or the St. Gothard.

In the evening I went back to Lexington,* which is a pretty little town with an excellent hotel, like all those in Virginia, where I for the first time saw a very simple and useful little machine, which I should call a *ventilator* or fly-chaser. It consists of several frames covered with cloth and with a fringe of feathers, hung at the right dis-

* Evidently it was Lexington where Arese was invited to the 4th of July banquet that so moved him.

tance above the table, and so arranged as to be set swinging by means of a cord, which an active negress never leaves idle. And apropos of negresses, may I be permitted to say that at Charlottesville I was shown a pretty one—although she was no longer young—who had beautified the last days of Jefferson. It appears that the celebrated author of the Declaration of Independence did not profess any great contempt for ebony, so long as it was solid and of good quality.

From Lexington I went to White Sulphur Springs, crossing the range of the Alleghanies, which divides the waters falling into the Atlantic from those falling into the Mississippi.

White Sulphur Springs is the most fashionable watering-place in Virginia; and there one meets people from every State in the Union. It is an establishment belonging to Mr. Coldwell (*sic*). His estate covers 5000 acres, and I have several times gone deer-hunting on it. The establishment could not be better laid out. It is in a small valley, and consists of 200 cottages nicely built of wood, a big dining-room 140 feet long and 30 feet wide, where there are at times 600 guests and room for them all, a ballroom and various shops. All this has been constructed after no plan, but bit by bit as there was need to enlarge the accommodations:

but this irregularity is not unattractive; the greater part of the houses are built along several lines or parallels, which cross one another; splendid trees are scattered here and there, the green carpet spread at their feet is cut up by little paths, and the whole impression is rather that of a camp. The table is pretty good, but people dine so fast and in such a disagreeable way, that you have no time, no leisure to appreciate the cook's talents. Late-comers take no more than 10 or 15 minutes. The entire dinner is served on one plate, roast beef, potatoes (inevitably), venison, currant jelly, ham, vegetables, eggs, what else besides? It makes you think of remnants from the master's table, all put together in one dish for the cat. It is a strange spectacle to see the cohort of waiters, white, black, and mulatto, running about and colliding while they serve that multitude of guests, while the patter of their rapid steps mingles with the clatter of plates and the rattle of knives and forks to disturb the forced silence of those eating.

Being now at White Sulphur Springs and having brought my diary up to date, let me say a few words about Virginia in general. The roads in Virginia are terrific, sometimes covered with great stones which it would not be fair to call gravel, but for the most part with a surface that holds the water, so that after rains, which are frequent in this region the stagecoach wheels sink into mud up to the axle, when the wind has dried the roads. The puddles are so deep that if there were others equal at the antipodes, it would be very easy to establish communications. When the ground is so marshy that there would not be any method of passing over it, the road is paved with little trees laid crossways side by side, so that the jouncing one enjoys is of extreme violence and liveliness. The only way to form any idea of it would be to drive a carriage down a stairway of very high and uneven treads. To the charm of the roadway must be added that of the carriages or diligences, which are called *Stages*. They have big bodies with six windows and three seats, into which are packed several unhappy travellers, who are just as comfortable as anchovies in a keg. There is no *outside* or imperial, only one place beside the driver. The large body is hung from 4 so-called springs, which are nothing but four pieces of iron set at right angles to the axles and holding up the vehicle by means of very long braces, whose movement might very easily make you, in a fatal moment of distraction, pop out of the door. You can hang on, grip on, cling on as much as you are able, you will land every evening shattered, bruised, done up!

The horses are good and in Eastern Virginia they are generally splendid and could go a great deal faster if the roads allowed it. The harnesses are clean and well made, and the drivers, though not so good as English coachmen, are still very much superior to those one has the displeasure of seeing on the seats of the diligences in France. Whenever I was able, I have taken the place next the driver and have chatted with him; and usually I have found agreeable men who have given me all the information I desired; men not lacking in education, not simply in regard to their own country, their government, industries, etc., etc., but also able to talk very sensibly about Europe and its geography and institutions.

The fare on the stages is twice as high as on those in Europe, with the added pleasure that in the same length of time you cover only half the distance. Virginia is incontestably one of the most beautiful countries one could find. It is a charming cross between the lower parts of Switzerland and the Black Forest. The greater part of it is covered with forests of oak and other trees of a fine dark green. Several mountain ranges cross it parallel to the Ocean. Their highest peaks rise to

6000 feet at the very most, so that it would be on the whole more correct to call them big hills rather than mountains. Usually the scenery is charming: the sole objection possible is that of monotony, because there are no lakes or big rivers to give variety. The soil is very fertile, and there are such pretty farms as might easily give one the taste for a pastoral life. Rye, wheat, Turkish grain which here is called *Indian corn,* and barley all grow to perfection. Fruit trees are not abundant, and since I arrived in Virginia I think I have not eaten a single piece of fresh fruit. In no European country, with the exception of Sicily, is hospitality practiced so well as in Virginia. In this respect one might say that the Golden Age has taken refuge in this lovely land. The stiffness you are vexed at finding elsewhere in the Union, is in Virginia replaced by friendliness; and it has happened to me more than once to get acquainted in the stage with people who have immediately invited me to their houses and have there treated me as well as they could a member of their own family. Other times, when I had asked information about things I was going to see, people have been so kind as to accompany me for distances of 28 and 30 miles.

The hotels in Virginia are excellent. When the

started for Guyandotte. At White Sulphur I got to know persons from various States, and in general I certainly found them very pleasant and well-bred, but with marked differences. The Northerners, for instance, are more formal, maybe more selfish and hard than the Easterners and Southerners, whose simplicity, candor, and *laisser aller* make it easy to overlook a slight tactlessness sometimes found in some of them.

The road from White Sulphur to Guyandotte provides the traveller not only with fine landscape, but also with other interesting things to see. You go through the pretty town of Lewisburg and from there to Blue Sulphur Springs, where the hotel has a good situation and is large enough to hold 250 people. Next I crossed the Sewell and the Gauley Mountains,* which contain rich coal mines. I visited the New River Cliffs, also called the Hawk's Nest. This is one of the most beautiful natural sights I have ever seen. Under almost perpendicular rocks a thousand feet high the New River flows rapidly through its very shut-in and very sombre valley. Excepting one portion of this valley which is full of boulders, the rest is covered with dark green trees. I saw this magnificent landscape at a most favorable moment—the setting

* In the text these names come out as Suvell and Coulce's.

sun shone full upon it: the warm and lively colors and shadows sharply cut by the edge of the mountains, enhanced even further the sublimity and poetry of a place which, of the sombre sort, is one of the loveliest to be found. It is very sad, however, for these poor Americans that they have no idea, no feeling of beauty. They do not see or imagine, they do not feel the truly lovely and grand. Not a single travel-book, not a guide-book or description, mentions this place. I believe that the Americans are fated not to know what to be pleased with themselves for. They never talk to you of their canals, of their railways, or of their steamboats, or of their navy, or of their various institutions; and certainly they would have reason to be proud and even very proud of all of them. But on the other hand they will rupture your ear-drums with their pictures, their statues, their monuments, their architecture, their army; and I give you my word of honor, all that has no more sense to it than nothing. On board a steamboat an officer from West Point, which we were then leaving, asked me if the school there was similar to those at Strasbourg and Metz. I told him: "Almost, sir; except that the one at West Point prepares for a skeleton army of 6,000 men, whereas the others prepare for one of 450,000 under arms."

When I was at West Point they waked me at 4 in the morning to see the guard changed. There were 20 privates and 1 petty officer. Instead of watching the guard come up, I myself went up on the terrace to see the sunrise and to enjoy at such a moment the view of a scene that God made for the purpose of giving us a good idea of his ability.

I went to see the Falls of the Kanawha, which are pretty enough without being anything remarkable. There is plenty of water, but it falls only 15 or 20 feet. I took in the pretty little town of Charlestown, Virginia,* and the Salt Works. In order to get the salt, pits have been dug close to the river, and the salt water is drawn from them by means of pumps worked by steam engines. Then by evaporation almost two million bushels of salt a year is made, and for the most part consumed in the West, where it is easy to ship it by the Kanawha, the Ohio, and the Mississippi. I also saw the Burning Spring, which is nothing more than a little escape of inflammable gas, which they light when they wish to. It is similar to Pietra Mala near Bologna, except that at Pietra Mala the gas is burning all the time, and much more of it.

* Now, of course, West Virginia; which is true also of Guyandotte specified below as being at the Western tip of Virginia.

I crossed the Kanawha by a ferry whose wheels were turned by a team of horses walking on a moving platform parallel to the wheels' axle, and which by means of a cog-wheel made the wheels of the boat revolve. A very simple machine, but very cleverly made, for it takes only a small space, and the crossing is made much quicker than on our European ferries.

I reached Guyandotte. The region I went through and the valley of the Kanawha are very well cultivated and scattered with charming and rich farms. At Guyandotte, at the extreme Western tip of Virginia, I left that beautiful country, not indeed with tears in my eyes, but certainly with great regret. If I had obeyed my feelings, I would have let the Ohio, the West, and the whole business, go to the devil, and returned to pass the Summer very agreeably in some corner of that lovely district: but I perceive that I am becoming American: "No Matter and goahead."* I went aboard a small steamboat at Guyandotte, and small though it was, still it was an American steamboat, which is to say well-made, pretty, clean, and comfortable.

* Printed precisely thus in the text.

III

Down the Ohio & Up the Mississippi to Saint Louis.

FROM Guyandotte I went to Cincinnati. The Ohio, which the French—the first colonizers thereabouts—had good reason for calling *la belle rivière,* is really a lovely river; and its banks covered with well-cultivated hills, fine farms, and growing towns, offer the traveller a beautiful and ever varied panorama. In the background there is often a second range of higher hills covered with magnificent woods. Unfortunately the rains had made the water muddy, and that detracted a good deal from the beauty of the landscape.

As we sailed past I saw the town of Portsmouth built on a high bank of the river; and its large shops and stores, the activity I noted there, gave me a good idea of the extent of its commerce. I could see Maysville,* too, but by moonlight, so that I cannot report much about it. During this short trip on the river I saw a large number of steamboats and flatboats going upstream and

* Which, however, is in Kentucky.

down, which showed me how progressive the region is. Cincinnati is the biggest town in Ohio, and I believe the biggest in the West, and is, so to say, the commercial metropolis of this section of the Union. The town is well situated and well built, rather in the style of Philadelphia (which is a very pretty style), and the astonishing things is that the town began its existence in 1808,* that in 1816 it had 16,000 inhabitants, in 1830 26,000, and today reckons 40,000.

There are many Germans and Alsatians there, about four-fifths of the population, and the sound of "Ja, mein Herr" in the streets, the number of cafés and beer-halls with German signs, the peasants dressed in black velvet and red coats with big silver buttons, for a moment carried me in imagination to Mannheim; and the similarity to Mannheim, even in the construction of the streets, made the dream seem more real. Mannheim, however, is a far better-looking town than Cincinnati.

I saw the outside of the house Mrs. Trollope built, whose architecture is as grotesque, as bizarre as the lady's writings. I took a ride on the surrounding hills, whence one enjoys a magnificent view, of the city and of the river, which traces

* Cincinnati dates from 1788.

a fine meandering design between Ohio and Kentucky. The country houses I saw are, on the exterior, similar in style to chalets in Switzerland. To do something quite unusual, I will put the date. Today is 16 July, Cincinnati, evening; and tomorrow I shall leave to cross Kentucky.

I left Cincinnati, bound for Lexington. On the shore of the Ohio opposite Cincinnati you find two sweet little towns separated by the little river Licking. I cannot refrain from remarking on the striking contrast between the cities on the two banks of the Ohio. Cincinnati is only some thirty years old and already has a population of 40,000 and is continually growing. Newport, which is in Kentucky and one of the oldest towns there, which has been in existence 160 years,* and which at the time of the War of Independence was a recruiting-station for the army of the republic, contains only 1600 inhabitants and is not growing at all. The comparison I have just made between the two towns can be extended (but not so strikingly) to the States of Ohio and Kentucky. And what is the cause of this? *Slavery.* Persons in Kentucky enlightened enough to see that, admit it and wish the system might be abol-

* Newport, Kentucky according to "The National Gazatteer" of L de Colange, New York, 1884, was founded in 1791 and was accordingly 46 years old at the time of Arese's visit.

ished, finding it not only unnecessary for their State, but even harmful.

From Newport I went to Georgetown, crossed Eagle Hill, and by way of Frankfort a charming little place well situated on the shore of the Kentucky, I came to Lexington (Kentucky), a pretty town that might be called rural, because the houses are so scattered about, that, excepting for the main street and one or two others, you would think you were looking rather at a group of country-houses than at a town properly so-called. I went to call on Mr. Henry Clay, the great man of the district for whom I had a letter. He has run for President and had a very good chance of being elected. Unfortunately he was not on his estate, but gone to town for the court sessions, or some such thing. I was shown over his house and his farm, the one very well built, comfortable, and handsomely furnished, and the other quite worthy to serve as a model for that kind of development. I was urged to return the next day to see Mr. Clay, but as that would have made me lose two days, I gave it up.

I admit that I have not the mania that impels the English and the Americans to get acquainted with famous men, not in order to realize their talents and merits, but merely so as to be able to say, "I am very well acquainted with him."* Really, unless you are very indiscreet, a first visit can never be long enough to enable you to judge of a man's qualities, but only perhaps of his patience. I think this way of becoming acquainted with a man through one call, is about the same as that adopted in visiting libraries, when one restricts himself to looking at the illustrations and the bindings of the books.

I left Lexington to go to Louisville, a pretty, well-built town on the Ohio, and very commercial. In the evening I went to the theatre, which was not bad, and the audience rather superior.

The most sincere and least bombastic Americans tell you that the country around Lexington is the garden of the United States: the others tell you it is the garden of the *world!* In reality it is very beautiful, but in a positive, numerical way, a money-beauty, in short an American beauty. It is a district of an unrivalled richness of soil, having fields covered with grain 5 feet tall. It is a district so flat as to give an excessively uniform and monotonous horizon. In one word, it is a district that appeals to the purse, not to the imagination. Before I leave Ohio and Kentucky, may I be permitted to make a few general remarks?

* In English in the text.

The State of Ohio is excellently cultivated, and the Germans who form the greater part of its population are the best settlers one could desire. I cannot say much about the interior, because I saw that State only from the steamboat and know nothing but the towns and their environs. Kentucky is also a very rich land agriculturally. There I saw fine fields and splendid forests, much more beautiful than those I had gone through in Virginia. In Virginia the virgin forests are, to tell the truth, a wall of leaves, trunks, and creepers, so compact and tight that it is quite impossible to penetrate them without an axe. To that must be added the fact of a great many trees felled either by lightning or by the wind, and rotting where they lie. In that sort of forest most of the trees are not of large size, because by being crowded together they prevent one another from growing as much as they might or would like to. The small amount of ground one can see is swampy, for the sun's rays have a hard time getting in to dry the soil. In those forests you often find all kinds and all sizes of snakes. Rattlesnakes are very common; their music is frequently heard. Parenthetically: that is one of the varieties of American music I care for least. In Kentucky on the other hand, the trees in the forests have plenty of room, so that they attain a gigantic size, and your eyes can see to a great distance in the forests, whose soil is covered with grass of a most lovely green. The first forests of that sort I saw made me suppose that men's hands had had something to do with their aspect, and I began to consider the desirability of virginity to be overrated, especially in regard to forests. But later I perceived that these also were virgin forests, and that restored some of my esteem for the quality.

The ways of the inhabitants of Ohio and even more those of the Kentuckians, are the contrary of those of the Virginians. It is the reverse of the medal; and if the Ocean separated the States, the difference could not be greater. Out of love for the truth I must say that as for people I had introductions to, I found them very nice; but the crowd travelling by steamboat or stage, the individuals encountered in hotels (and that takes in all classes, for in America and especially in the West everybody travels)—I must say that the crowd is badly brought-up, rude, uncivil, disagreeable, stinking: in a word, they are animals of an inferior type dressed like men. I may add to this that the Kentuckians have an exaggerated conceit; and if the Americans themselves, who in general are more than sufficiently conceited, make the same criticism I make, one is really forced to say that this fault in the dear inhabitants of Kentucky surpasses every extreme. I cannot resist copying here a sign I read where it hung in the reading-room of the best hotel in Louisville, perhaps the most important and busiest city in Kentucky:

"Gentlemen are particularly requested not to "deface or remove the files of Newspapers from "the Readingroom; waste paper can be had on ap- "plying at the bar!"*

In spite of this so clear and solemn notice, not a single newspaper had been respected; and you must remember that the season for fevers and other sicknesses had not yet begun.

I took a steamboat at Louisville to go down the Ohio, a fine river though a trifle monotonous. The water, which generally is clear and green, was unfortunately, during my voyage, muddy; and as it was too low for running the rapids, the steamboat went through a canal dug for that purpose parallel to the Ohio. It is 2 miles long, and is connected with the river by 4 big locks, one after the other. 32 minutes, watch in hand, was enough to work those huge gates—about the length of time taken by the stages to change horses. Un-

* In English in the text.

lucky they who are condemned to travel by land in America! But on the other hand, lucky those who can travel by water, either in sailboats on the sea, or on steamboats on the rivers, and even by boat on the canals!

After the canal, the banks of the Ohio for some 100 miles are handsome, being high and clothed with woods; but then they become flat and monotonous. Now and then houses are to be seen, cultivated fields, and little villages honored with the name of towns. At Trinity you pass from the Ohio into the Mississippi. Because of rains, the waters of the two rivers at the junction were equally muddy. So I could not enjoy the sight of their two currents—one usually clear and the other always turbid—flowing along without mingling. Nevertheless I was able to form some idea of it by seeing several small streams whose water was as clear as crystal, empty into the Mississippi and keep their own color as far away as eye could follow.

The Mississippi is an imposing river. It might be called a prolonged lake. Its banks are in general flat and covered with poplars, so that it reminded me of our own Po. Its current is pretty strong; sometimes it is even 5 to 6 miles an hour. Some hundreds of miles below Saint Louis you begin to see bluffs; and I must mention one called the Tower* because of its shape, which stands in the water like an island. The shores, which are forever eaten away and carried off by the river, and the enormous number of floating trees, give the impression of a perpetual flood. On the banks, in the midst of forests, you see plantations and small towns, whose names I cannot be blamed for not having charged my memory with, for frequently two or three log-houses bear the name of some great European capital, or another name famous in history. 12 miles below Saint Louis you see Jefferson Barracks, where the government keeps several regiments to protect the country thereabouts against Indians.

One remarkable thing is that between Louisville and Saint Louis, a distance of 500 to 600 miles, I saw the wrecks of at least 25 boats. When I asked an explanation from persons familiar with the region, they told me that on the average about forty a year are either run aground or burn or blow up. Since there are 400 to 500 steamboats in the West, this gives the terrifying proportion of 10 percent. The greater number run on sandbanks or are ripped open by what the Americans call *snags* and the French *chicots*: that is to say,

* Grand Tower Island in Perry County, Missouri.

trees carried by the current. Sometimes the roots of these get caught in the river bed and the top sticks up in the air until in winter the boughs are cut off by ice, so that the end of the trunk is just on the surface of the water. These are not dangerous to a boat going downstream, because they yield to pressure; but when they are a foot or two under the surface and the pilot of a boat going upstream does not see them in time to avoid them, they make a hole in the boat, which sinks at once. More than once these snags have been known to protrude into passengers' staterooms. What a pleasant surprise!

There is a mistaken idea that the usual cause of steamboats' exploding is the habit, the mania for racing. I cannot possibly share that opinion. When the boats are going, the captain is on the bridge, the mate at the wheel, the two engineers in their place, everybody where he ought to be, and an accident is almost impossible. I have observed all this more than once. And when another vessel comes into sight and has been recognized, especially if she is swift, you would think the trumpet had blown for battle. I believe the general reason for disaster is the following: steamboats stop very frequently to take and discharge passengers and freight. Sometimes they stop longer than they expected to, the steam in the boilers condenses, and the water diminishing on that account permits the upper part of the boiler to get red hot: the cold water afterwards introduced suddenly with the first stroke of the piston causes the boiler to explode; and then the whole vessel is torn apart, people are hurled into the air, scalded, wounded, crippled, and what remains of them goes to feed the fishes. But all that does not bother the Americans, so long as you can go and go quickly: and in view of their carelessness and indifference, I cannot conceive why there are not even more accidents.

I was on board the "Tempest," reading in the saloon, when somebody came hurrying to tell me to go up on deck and see a steamboat that had sunk while she was trying to help another get refloated. As we were making 16 knots, instead of going on the bridge, I went on the roof in order to see farther (the vessels in the West do not usually have an open deck, but they have two covered decks and a roof), and the first thing I saw was fire on that roof, with flames 3 or 4 feet high. I at once yelled, "Fire aboard," a terrible cry, but a magic one on anything that floats. Everybody began rushing about, they came up on the roof where I was, the captain ahead. The stewards had put mattresses to air on the roof and the sparks incessantly pouring from the smokestacks had set them afire. The mattresses were thrown into the water, and all was in order again. But for a lucky chance the "Tempest" five minutes later would have ended her career: the roof was covered with canvas waxed and varnished, so that the fire would not have taken long to spread to the whole vessel. For the sake of future voyagers I hoped that the captain would swear, at least that he would scold and forbid putting any more mattresses on the roof; but he did not say a single word.

But something that gave me a much more disagreeable shock on the same boat was this:—a miserable German who had nothing in the world except the sack on his back, had been taken aboard gratis on condition of his helping load wood: very nice! But what was not very nice is that the poor devil having been ill in the night and unable to load the darned wood, next morning was pitilessly put ashore at the first landing, to get out of his plight as best he could. Unfortunately this was not generally known until the man was already ashore and the rowboat that took him had returned, so that it was too late to help him in any way. An incident much more serious, and really atrocious and barbarous, took place on the Mississippi only some two months ago. During the night a steamboat, which if I am not mistaken was named the "Bensherod,"* caught fire. The crew, seeing that the fire was spreading horribly fast, took to the rowboats without troubling themselves to ring the alarm and warn the unfortunate passengers, who were awakened by the flames or by water. About 180 persons were killed, and only 10 or 12 had the good luck to save themselves. But the last word in shameless atrociousness was the behavior of the captain of another steamboat, who when the next morning he passed through the débris of the burned boat and saw several people that had been fortunate enough to cling to it, not only did not try to rescue them, but did not even stop his engines and thus ruthlessly submerged the poor souls whom fire and water had spared! I would not believe such horrors had I not read the details in all the American newspapers.

The city of Saint Louis is built on an inclined plane, so that when you arrive there by river, it is like an amphitheatre. Six years ago this town scarcely existed,† and now it has a population of

* He was slightly mistaken. She was called the "Ben Sherrod."
† Possibly; but it had been there seventy-four years.

almost 18,000, and the day I arrived there I counted 48 steamboats at the dock, and they were magnified steamboats, fabulous in size and luxuriousness. I went over the "Saint Louis," which has 8 boilers and 2 engines, a tonnage of 1000, and very often 400 passengers on board.

The most remarkable thing at Saint Louis, and the thing that has caused the rapid development of its commerce and wealth, is the American Fur Company,* founded by Mr. Astor, who is now at this moment the richest man in America, that is to say, in the United States. He is said to be worth 30 million dollars. This immense enterprise, whose object is to cover the forests and the prairies of the Far West, is divided into two sections: one, under the direction of Mr. Ramsay Crooks, takes care of the Mississippi and the Great Lakes; the other, of the region extending from the Missouri to the Rocky Mountains, and it has Mr. Chouteau at its head. I had the good fortune to meet both of these very worthy men, without whose help it would have been quite impossible for me to un-

* The very excellent book "The American Fur Trade of the Far West," Capt. (now Gen.) Hiram Martin Chittenden, New York, 1902, p. 364, says, " . . . 1834, when the Northern Department, retaining the name of American Fur Company, was sold to a company of which Ramsay Crooks was the principal partner, and the Western Department to Pratte, Chouteau and Company of St. Louis."

dertake the trip I intended to make. This huge company has several steamboats and several thousand men in its service. Mr. Crooks was one of the fearless travellers that first crossed the American continent and the Rocky Mountains and made an outpost on the shore of the Pacific Ocean and called it Astoria. It was destroyed by specious pretexts raised by the jealousy of England—a thing that happens very frequently to new colonies. The trade is widespread, and would be far more so, if Europe permitted the importation of American pelts and furs.

The proverb says that when you speak of a wolf you will see his ears or his tail, and sometimes it is true. Yesterday I wrote a few lines about steamboats' exploding, and an hour since I looked on at one of the horrible spectacles. I was in the offices of the American Fur Company, which are on the levee, when an explosion sounding like that of a mine, was heard. A vast mass of white smoke, or rather steam, terrible cries, human bodies, boxes and bales of merchandise, planks floating downstream, all this tossed about pell-mell, left no doubt about what sort of accident had occurred. There were 7 men dead and several severely wounded. I saw one whose skin had been loosened by boiling water, and what was detached from his breast hung down nearly to his thighs. It was dreadful to see. Several small boats were immediately launched and went swiftly down the river to pick up the victims the current was carrying away. The damage to the steamboat was not so great as I expected. The explosion took place forward and on the sides, and there was only one plank missing from the upper deck. This time again the boiler blew up at the moment of putting off after a short stop. As usual, it was entirely the captain's fault. Yet the law takes no notice of all these fatalities, and no more does public opinion. Every one out here is so used to it that nobody pays any attention.

I talked of this accident to the captain of another steamboat, who blamed his colleague. But when I said I was amazed that there is no law about such things, he replied: "If there were a law, either it would not be enforced, or if it were, nobody would be willing to be a captain. Do the captains beg passengers to travel in their boats? If they do travel in them, it is at their own risk and peril, which after all are shared by the captain too."

There, it seems to me, is logical reasoning for you! One can imagine nothing comparable to the apathy and indifference of those gentlemen—an apathy, as a matter of fact, that is most contagious. I asked the captain of the steamboat that was going to take me in several days to Council Bluffs, how many days we should require to get there, and he replied: "9 days is more than enough; but we must reckon at least 12 on account of accidents." "What do you mean by accidents?" "Damage," he answered, "that might be done to the boat by running aground. In that case, you have to count the time required to refloat her." "Do you expect to run aground?" "I don't expect anything; but you have to take that into account, because the water is low and the rapids very strong." "Why make the trip, then?" "Because I have freight I must carry up there." Persuaded by the force and reasonableness of his arguments, I several days later went aboard his boat, as a bale of merchandise that also had to be carried up there.

The "St. Peter," on which I was to travel not being yet entirely loaded, I had to remain several days in Saint Louis. I took advantage of this to go hunting, and to explore the environs, a monotonous country, but very fertile and magnificently wooded.

I visited an Indian tribe living a few leagues from the town. They were what are called hereabouts civilized. Thank you, thank you a thousand times for that sort of civilization! Nothing more degrading to human nature can be imagined than those wretches who have adopted no part of civilization except its liquor, its gunpowder, and its s——.* 7 or 8 miserable buffalo-skin tents supported by trees, poor samples of horses, thin and galled grazing nearby, some women preparing deerskins or taking care of hideous, stark naked babies, a few saddles, a few guns, a few clumsy utensils, and empty bottles! That made up the colony of the Indians they call *civilized*. Their get-up is the most grotesque you could hope to see. It is a combination of the white man's and their own; and all of it dirty and disgusting. Some of them speak a few words of bad English, about the same kind I flatter myself that I speak. These unfortunates have learned neither to cultivate the ground, nor to raise cattle. The game they kill provides their food, and the skins they sell are exchanged for brandy, gunpowder, tobacco for the men, beads of glass or Chinese vermilion for the women. This tribe is what remains of the Delawares formerly so numerous and so strong.

The Saint Louis theatre is one of the best-looking I have seen in the United States, and certainly the audience is superior to those else-

* Abbreviation in text.

where in America. Theatrical shows are more a part of the habits of the town than in the other cities, where the population, being of English or Dutch descent, cares less for such amusements than the French creoles. The performance was good; there was even a little ballet. And certainly in Europe you could not find such a good theatre and so pretty in a town of 18,000 inhabitants. I like Saint Louis too well to speak of its Museum; but still one must be just—what can you expect from a town only ten years old? The people there are hospitable and have the amiability and the politeness which one would look for in vain among their neighbors the Kentuckians. The one execrable thing in Saint Louis is the hotels, which are filthy, disgusting, and quite adapted to hardening travellers about to venture into the Far West, beyond where white men live.

IV

Up the Missouri to Council Bluffs.

At last the boat was ready and I left. The deck gave an idea of the sort of voyage the boat was setting out on: there were anchors, chains, piles of rope, huge poles, planks, axes, and a large beam to serve as a shore to hoist up the boat if it grounded—a precaution which the sequel proved to be necessary. Except me, everybody aboard belonged to the American Fur Company. Some of them were heads of factories and depots, but the largest number was made up of hunters, trappers, and voyageurs, mostly French, or to speak more precisely, of French extraction, and well assorted for giving an idea of the shades of human skin in Europeans—creoles, negroes, mulattos of different degrees, half-breeds, and who knows what not? A strict moralist or a Jesuit would term them lost souls; but judging them less severely, one finds them good boys full of life and activity, spry, in good trim, shrewd, and above all preferring whisky to God, and not fearing the Devil so much as the Indians' bullets and arrows. Certainly the life bristling with danger, fatigue, and privation, which they lead for 11 months a year, gives them the right to make up to themselves for all that in the one month left them, during which they conscientiously follow the rule of spending everything they have earned the rest of the year. And why, after all, should they economize, not being very certain of coming back another time?

Despite distance, time, and the crossing of races, one recognizes in them the type of the Paris gamin: the same good humor under all circumstances, the same physical and moral elasticity: and I not only was pleased to see, but I enjoyed seeing that the *chahut** is not unknown in the New World.

Although their costumes are as bizarre as their behavior, they are not lacking in coquetry, especially in regard to their hair. Some like it very smooth and shiny like the Indians', others like to have long ringlets on their shoulders, for curling papers are not unknown among these men of the mountains and the forests. Their good-byes to their friends and acquaintances come to the levee to see them off on a journey they might well never return from, were much more comic than touch-

* This is printed "châute." The chahut was an unseemly dance, a predecessor of the can-can.

ing. It was like the conversations you hear in Carnival between the boxes and the gallery at the Franconi theatre.

The country from Saint Louis to where the Missouri enters the Mississippi is nothing startling; little towns and villages are scattered here and there on the river banks. I had supposed it impossible to find muddier, dirtier water than that of the Mississippi, but when I saw the Missouri, I was undeceived. I saw that it is the Missouri water that dirties the Mississippi, which is clean and clear above the junction. Our mountain streams after a Summer storm are as limpid as spring-water in comparison to the Missouri, which is almost chestnut in color: and the amount of earth and sand it carries is so great that a glass filled with its water at night is found in the morning to be one fourth sediment. And yet the water does not taste; it even is wholesome; it only requires a little courage to swallow it for a few days, and then one has the habit.

The currents of the two rivers run alongside each other quite a distance before mingling. I have seen small rivers whose lovely clear water flowed in a solid stream through the Missouri, as if they avoided soiling their purity by touching the dark and muddy water of the big river.

The town of St. Charles makes a good appearance. After passing it you still for some while see villages. But farther up there are only log-houses, which is to say huts built of tree trunks. Soon after there are no dwellings, and will be no more to see before reaching Fort Leavenworth. The banks of the Missouri are flat and wooded. Only once in a while you see some limestone rocks which never are so much as a hundred feet high. One of these rocks, higher than the rest, which has a sort of cave in it, is known to the people thereabouts as *Tavern Rock,* and serves as a refuge for the crews of the flat-boats that go up and down the river.

Our trip as far as Fort Leavenworth went very well, although our keel frequently dragged along sand-bars, and now and then snags rubbed the sides of our boat. But we ran aground only one trifling time, and a very short while sufficed to set us afloat again. The next day a great roguish snag struck violently against the steamboat and water entered, and then the pump was working day and night, which is not particularly amusing, both because of the noise it makes, and because of the consequences that might ensue.

It would be perfectly impossible to have a captain better grounded, more active, more prudent, and at the same time more persistent than the one commanding the "St. Peter." He is a Mr. Pratte (son of the general of the same name), who is in charge of all the steamboats of the American Fur Company, of which he is one of the partners. It is purely to oblige his associates and to amuse himself that he is willing to take the job of commanding boats on the runs where a good captain is indispensable. He was one of the first to go in a steamboat as far up the Missouri as the Yellowstone. I will say nothing of his good nature, because having been overwhelmed by him with kindness and thoughtfulness, I should be too partial a judge; I will leave that to others who have also had the good fortune of knowing him. Their judgment—I have no doubt—will be the same as mine. But I really cannot refrain from speaking of the amazing cleverness of the pilots, most of whom are half-breeds. In many places the river was so clustered with snags that it really seemed as if it would be absolutely impossible to find a way among them. The difficulty was augmented by the strength of the current, which made the effect of the tiller almost imperceptible. Despite all of which our pilot has invariably steered his boat with the same precision an able coachman would guide his vehicle with. Sometimes the danger of collision was so great that everybody was ready with axes and all other necessary implements in hand. But the only thing that was really alarming for a moment was that 4 men on board were taken with terrible colic and vomiting. As there were in Saint Louis still some few cases of cholera or cholerine, we thought that was what ailed them.

What was very strange was that although everybody has that idea, not a single mouth has pronounced the fatal word. At the moment I write this, three of the men are nearly well and the fourth is dying of an intestinal inflammation, according to what the captain tells me, and he is the ship's doctor.

Fort Leavenworth is the last American post. It has a regiment of dragoons and artillery to keep the savages respectful. Some wretched barracks and a second-rate blockhouse is all there is to what is called the military establishment. A long time before we reached the fort, there were no more log-houses of white men; and soon after the last one we began to see Indians, who ran down to the shore to watch the steamboat go by. The evening of that day we called at a post of the American Fur Company and landed the boss of the trading station, which is on the river bank. The boat was instantly flooded with savages, to whom tobacco and brandy were given. They greeted the boss of the station affectionately, wringing his hand and calling him "Papá, papá." They played cards with great enthusiasm and even passion, and remained on board very late that night; and three young Indian women remained on board all night! . . . and with the consent of the chief of the tribe. It was the tribe of Kickapoos.

The next day we saw a village of Sacs and Foxes, and that night we stopped at Serpent Noir,* a place inhabited by Iowas, of whom we saw a few. At Fort Leavenworth there was a big gathering of savages because it so happened that several chiefs of different tribes were there then, who, on account of being on their way to Washington to see the President, were all in their finest costumes. But fine as they were, I much preferred seeing them in lithographs. The first time I saw Indians and was really, so to say, in contact with them, they caused me to feel such disgust and fright (in Italian I would say *ribrezzo*, but I do not know the equivalent word in French) as seemed unconquerable; and I should never have suspected that within three months I should be glad to sleep between two Indians (males, of course), side by side so as to keep warm during a night of North wind.

* On the site of St. Joseph there was a post called Blacksnake Hills. Chittenden, p. 949.

Their heads are shaved except for one little lock or a little queue, painted red and black, their faces too painted in the same colors, and all shiny from the grease that covered them. They are simply hideous. On their heads they wear a lot of small feathers of various colors, and three or four very long ones, standing up or hanging: to that they add glass beads and pieces of deers' horn or bone; all of which has some special meaning, and usually one referring to their own exploits, that is, the number of men they have killed or the number of horses they have stolen. In their ears, or around them, they wear rings or strings of beads, under the weight of which ornaments their ears bend down and sometimes are completely closed, exactly like those of a hunting-dog.

These last few days we have seen several flocks of parakeets,* but of a small variety. They were entirely green except their yellow heads. We have also seen a number of wild turkeys, which are very much like our European turkeys, but larger and of a very dark chestnut color and with a bunch of thick hair, like horsehair, in the middle of the breast. At Black Snake I saw some ducks

* These must have been Carolina Parrots (Centurus carolinensis) according to Audubon's "Birds of America," 1842, vol. IV, p. 305.

much bigger than ours in Europe, with white, brown, and black plumage. In this part of the country they call them *bustards,* but they are totally different from the bustards I saw in Africa.

In conversations on board people told me two stories that show how insufficient the laws are in the United States, especially when public opinion is against them. A party of gamblers worked the Ohio and the Mississippi steamboats with great success. They reached Pittsburg (or Vicksburg, I don't remember which) and there the poor devils did very nicely—in fact too nicely, for the inhabitants massacred them in the most ruthless manner, and only two or three of the whole lot were able to run away. No legal attempt was made to punish a crime that cost the lives of a dozen people. The second story referred to Saint Louis. There somebody accused a negro of having tried to attack the constable, and another officer arrested him. As they were taking him to jail, the negro killed the two of them and got away. He was caught and put in jail. Before his trial friends and relatives of the constable went to the keeper and ordered him to turn the negro over to them. They got the poor chap and took him out of town to where they had a stake all ready. While they were lighting the fire, an elderly man remarked that the negro was going to be tried and would be found guilty and executed, and that consequently there was no need whatever for them to dirty their hands with blood, since the courts were there to see that he got the punishment his crime deserved. The answer he got to this was that if he didn't clear out right away, he would make a pair with the negro; and the honest man was obliged to pocket his philanthropy and trust to his legs, for otherwise he would certainly have shared the fate of the poor negro, who was cruelly burned slowly to death, without the public's trying to prevent it. Not the slightest attempt was made by the law to catch and punish the guilty. This took place in the Spring of 1836. I mention these two facts, because though I did not see them, they were related to me by persons seriously deserving to be believed. If one attempted to tell of all the outrages of that sort which have occurred, he would never finish.

To get back to my trip: when the boat stops at the trading posts, which are also called forts, it is very odd to see the hunters, trappers, and so on, who, before the boat is fast to the landing, jump over the railings and overrun the stockade, the field, and the house from cellar to garret. Maize, potatoes, everything, is looted, including dogs and cats; and all this is done in a flash, before the captain has time to call them back on board.

After 11 days on the Missouri we reached the Council Bluffs, which take their name from the fact that they used to be the place that served as a rendezvous for the Indians of the various tribes in the vicinity, who met there to hold war-councils.* Today it is a trading post of the American Fur Company and consists of only three or four little houses and a few warehouses, the whole enclosed by a poorly built stockade. It is there that the Indians come to exchange furs and hides for cloth, beads, powder, lead, guns, and whisky, which they prefer to all the rest and which is given them in spite of a law forbidding it. It is furnished them not through cupidity, but for the sake of *morality* and in the *interest of the Indians,* or so one is told! (At Yellowstone the Company can buy a horse for two bottles of whisky, and it sells whisky to these men for 32 dollars a gallon). This is the explanation given: the Indians, they say, are mad for alcohol. If we do not furnish it to

*Chittenden says (p. 947), "The particular situation always known in those early years as Council Bluffs was twenty-five miles above the modern city of that name, and on the opposite side of the river about where the little town of Calhoun is now located. On the 3rd of August, 1804, Lewis and Clark held a council there with the Oto and the Missouri Indians and gave the name from the circumstance."

them, the ones in the North will go to get it from the Hudson Bay Company (an English company and therefore a rival of the American company's), and those in the South will go East to buy it at the first white settlement. To do either they must spend a long, long time, during which they abandon their families, do no hunting, and sell their goods to somebody else (and there you have the true explanation).

The law was introduced in Congress by Mr. Cass, then Secretary of War,* and one of the heroes of the "Temperance Society;" and at the same time he got a law passed to stop the issuing of whisky to the sailors and the soldiers. That law had a good effect on the sailors while they were at sea; but upon the soldiers its effect has been disastrous. When the troops in a garrison depended on their ration of liquor, it very seldom happened that there were men in the guardhouse for drunkenness. It could hardly have been otherwise, because the soldiers of the American Army being in forts on the farthest Indian frontiers, had no means of procuring spirituous liquors. But no sooner was the law in operation than charitable souls who cared more for money than for the progress of the "Temperance Society," estab-

* Cass was appointed Secretary of War in 1831.

lished themselves near the forts, and they sell the soldiers as much whisky not as they can drink, but as they can pay for. The result is that the troops (if one can honor the American soldier with that name) get drunk, do not come back when called to quarters, get tired of being arrested, and desert; and it frequently happens that there are not enough men to do the work of the fort.

It is very curious to see that at each of the trading posts there has been started a manufactory, so to speak, of half-breeds. Every petty clerk or apprentice has his *squaw* (the name given Indian women), who usually wears her native costume, but as richly ornamented as possible, for Indian women also measure love by the presents given them.

When we reached Council Bluffs there was an Indian standing on high ground a good hundred feet above river level. In three bounds he was down, as easily and neatly as if he had been a deer. I stayed two days at Council Bluffs to get mounts, equipment, and provisions. Finally I left there with three horses, one of which carried me, another a half-breed who was to be my guide as far as the Vermilion River,* which flows about sixty

* The Vermilion enters the Missouri from the North in what is now Clay County, South Dakota.

miles above the large Sioux River, and the third was loaded with pork, biscuits, corn, coffee, sugar, and two kettles. A third man came along with us, engaged by the half-breed. We left the Otoes and the Pawnees, and started off toward the Grande Prairie.

[V]

On Horseback to the Vermilion River & a Visit in a Sioux Village.

After riding some leagues, we met a wolf which I followed trying in vain to shoot it. We passed a lake that was covered with a swarm of ducks. There we also saw masses of herons and a pelican. But the prairie alongside was too marshy for us to dare trust ourselves on it so as to fire at those birds. We rode all day and camped that night near another smaller lake. The day had been excessively hot. The night was horrible, without a minute of sleep because we were so tormented by the *marangouens,* which are a sort of giant mosquito, by the *brûlots,* another species that takes its name from the agreeable effect produced by its sting,* and by a hideous flock of other insects, which devoured us all night long. In the morning our bodies looked as if they were covered with an eruption.

Before sunrise we were afoot. We looked for our horses: but they had vanished. To defend our-

* The name "brûlot" would suggest that the bite burned hard.

selves against the mosquitoes we had made a fire and smothered it with fresh grass to make a smudge, and then had gone to bed to windward, so that we got all the smoke. The horses, which had been fastened with the head of one to the tail of another, had come around behind us so as to get the advantage of the smoke too. But as soon as there was no more of it, they were so distressed by the insects that they must have gone elsewhere to try to find some relief. Not discovering them, we surmised that some Pawnees or Omahas, then at war with each other, must have passed, and as those brave fellows do not recognize the rights of neutrals, had stolen our horses. We almost pardoned them for that, seeing they had not permitted themselves to play any more serious jokes: and then, after having run about for two hours, we finally found the horses, and got started.

The second and third days we travelled without any further troubles, excepting for the insects which kept us in a state of continual fever. We saw deer and fallow deer,* without going near them because we did not wish to lose too much

* Arese says "des cerfs et des daims," and probably means by "cerfs" either Cervus Canadensis (common deer) or Cariacus Virginianus (red deer), and by "daims" Cervus (dama) dama (fallow deer).

time. We met several more wolves during the daytime, but we had grown used to those, for every night they came in packs to visit our little camp, without causing us to stir from under our covers. Only the first night we did amuse ourselves by firing a few shots at them; but when the novelty had worn off, we economized our powder and bullets.

The fourth day in the evening, while our salt pork was cooking, we noticed smoke far away. We at once made a thousand guesses, and although we all agreed that there was nothing to fear, still, without any one's suggesting it, we put tinder into our muskets, bullets instead of shot, and in spite of mosquitoes and company, we let the fire go out, so that our blaze should not be reciprocally seen. We tethered the horses carefully, close by; and next morning an hour before daylight, we were in the saddle. That day we crossed what is called the Grande Prairie, which is from 36 to 40 miles long and entirely level. The wind moving the deep grass almost made me believe I was in the middle of the ocean. Usually prairies are not level, but gently rolling; and in the little valleys formed by the rolling there flow streams, larger or smaller. And those are among the major discomforts of a trip across the prairies, because the little rivers have a very bad bottom, and the horses have to be taken over riderless, to avoid the danger of their getting stuck in the mud. You have it up to your knees, and water up to your belly. And since there are 10 or 12 of them to ford every day and it would waste too much time to undress and dress for each one, you stay soaked from morning till night.

Early on the fifth day we reached a village of the Omahas. They had all left for fear of the Pawnees, and we were the owners of the village, which was surrounded by a moat and a stockade, and which we, so to speak, took by storm. For we opened the stockade, hatchet in hand, and made a little bridge over the moat, to lead our horses across. The village consisted of a dozen large lodges, of the kind generally built, of tree trunks cemented with mud. They are round, and inside all around against the wall lean benches made of rush, which, by covering them with a buffalo robe, serve as well for beds. Inside there are also eight tree trunks to hold up the roof made of bark covered with earth. The roof is conical in shape, with a hole in the middle to let out smoke. You go into the house through a sort of little corridor. The one we occupied was about 40 feet in diameter and was meant to hold at least 200 people. Besides the wigwams, there were some constructions resembling large cages made of stout poles, for the purpose of shutting up horses when a surprise by enemies threatened.

In the house we chose for our abode, fastened to one of the beams supporting the roof, there was an arrow with a scalp and a small bunch of wood and dry grass. I asked an explanation from the half-breed, who told me that there was a religious idea attached to the little bunch of grass, just as there is to our relics, and that the owners of the place had left it in charge of the enemy scalp and of Medicine. The Indians call everything that is sacred or extraordinary Medicine. In one corner of the house there was a heap of large stones, and he told me the savages used those for taking steam baths. For that purpose they build very small wigwams of buffalo hide, then they heat the stones red hot in the fire, put them into the little wigwam, throw water over them, close the place tightly, and thus produce steam thick enough to smother any one but an Indian. I also found a whole bunch of feathers of eagles, swans, and other birds, to be used either as head decoration or for arrows. I used them to clean my good old German pipe.

We went up on the roof to see whether we

could discover anything in the distance; and having found that everything was perfectly quiet all around us and far away, we lighted our fire inside the cottage [chaumière], we gathered some maize (the Omahas are among the small number of those that begin to raise crops), and that was our repast. We filled our sacks, which were empty, and we allowed our horses to stuff themselves out of shape, after we ourselves were gorged. After having smoked a good pipe and taken another look around from the roof, to reassure ourselves that we should not have to do the honors of our abode to anybody, we took advantage of the coolness inside it to get a bit of sleep; and then we started along again.

An hour later we reached the Omaha River.* We sounded it in various spots, trying to find a ford. Impossible! While the half-breed and I were busy making a raft, the other hunter, who went on sounding, discovered a place where the water came only up to our shoulders. We rendered our costumes as simple as possible, and by means of several trips we succeeded in carrying our saddles, our blankets, provisions, clothing, etc., across on our heads. We got our horses to swim,

* Omaha Creek was to the West of Wahkah (now Woodbury) County, Iowa.

and as soon as we were over the river, we immediately started on again.

Now I must explain what a *cageux*, the sort of raft we made, is. It is put together of four pieces of wood formed into a square with their ends overlapping, fastened with ropes or stalks of creepers. Over this one ties a buffalo robe, and on that are placed the baggage and the hydrophobes, which is to say, those who do not know how to swim. The whole contraption is floated and a man or two men swim and push it; or else they tow it by a rope between their teeth; and thus the *cageux* crosses the river.

The sixth day in the morning we halted in a prairie beside a small river we had just crossed; and the fire we lighted began to set fire to the prairie. The half-breed said: "Hurry up. Let's put it out." But as we were to leeward and the wind was strong, I begged him to do nothing. Although it was not the proper season, this prairie had taken fire easily because of not having burned the year before. The dry straw caught first and spread the flames to the grass just beginning to grow. It was beautiful to see: at the beginning you might have said an immense line of battle keeping up well-sustained firing. It was a sea of flame.

After dinner we reached the banks of the Missouri. We went up on the bluff and made signals to a camp of Sioux on the other side of the river, in which was the family of the half-breed who was travelling with me.* They sent us a canoe in which we crossed the stream, while the horses swam over. As the place where we crossed was farther downstream than the camp, the half-breed and I entered the woods, to go there on foot. A half-hour after going into the woods we heard a strange sort of crying. The half-breed told me it would be some Indian mourning for a dead person. Sure enough we soon reached a small wigwam in front of which sat an old man weeping or crying in a way to take the skin off his windpipe and not to leave a bit on the ears of whosoever was unlucky enough to pass by there. As soon as he recognized my half-breed, he dried his tears, lighted his pipe, shook hands with us (a friendly custom the savages have learned from the whites), and we smoked his pipe by turns; which is equivalent to our handshaking, with the unhappy dif-

* The half-breed, as we shall soon see, was named what Arese writes Dixon. We already know that the Vermilion River was where they had been aiming. Almost at that spot Chittenden places "Dickson's Post," one of the fur stations. Jean Nicholas Nicollet in the report he made with his topographical map published by Congress in 1843, says that he engaged William Dixon as a guide in 1839, spelling the name as Arese spells it.

ference that after having smoked a pipe with an Indian you can count on him, whereas such is not, alas! always the case after having shaken a European's hand. The half-breed asked for a drink, and the old man gave us a cup of water. Then he told the half-breed that half the lodges were empty, because the occupants had died of smallpox,* and that when we arrived he had been mourning for his son who had died that morning. The half-breed asked for news of his own family. Fortunately he had no loss to regret. With that good news we reached the camp at six in the evening, where we unhappily verified what the old man had told us, for out of 25 or 30 lodges a good half were entirely empty.

There was nothing I desired more than to leave the next morning for the St. Pierre River;† but that was impossible for two good reasons: first, my horses were tired and needed a 3 or 4 days' rest; secondly, the Sioux whom the half-breed intended to make my guide, had left on an expedition with twelve other warriors of the tribe. He was expected back at any moment. So, not being

* 1837 was the terrible smallpox year among the Indians. It must not be supposed that those left of them continued to die off at the same rate.

† The Saint Pierre or St. Peter's River is the Minnesota at present.

able to leave by myself, either for going ahead or for going back, I had no choice except to blow out my brains or to remain placidly with the Sioux, in spite of the smallpox raging violently in the tribe. I took the latter course, and I took it absolutely, for I bothered no more about smallpox than if such a thing never had existed in this world. I was put up at the half-breed's house.

And here I shall say a couple of words in regard to him. A certain Dixon, Scottish by birth, came during the last century to the St. Pierre River, where he settled among the Indians to trade in furs. His courage, his intrepidity, and his intellectual force gained for him the confidence of the Indians he lived among, to such a point that they chose him for chief in a war against the Americans. Though he fought against men of his own color and against civilization, still Dixon behaved like a decent man and did not deceive those who had taken him into their tribe and made so much of him. He took a Sioux wife, by whom he had several children; among them William Dixon about whom I am speaking. William Dixon, son of a white man and an Indian woman, was a fine mixture of the good points of the two races, for he added to the results of a good bringing-up among white men, the instinct, the perspicacity, and the keen senses of the savage. Though the son of a white man and educated among white people, William leaned much more toward the Indians, both as to his tastes and habits, and as to his affections and sympathies. When he talked of wars between the Americans and the Indians, it was always in favor of the latter that he spoke. However, the same is true of all half-breeds. I know his family, and it is really what is called a patriarchal family. I am writing these few lines in his loghouse. I have been received in his home as well as any one can be received anywhere: and when I left it, I was overwhelmed with presents, such as moccasins, pipes, and other Indian curiosities, which will always be an agreeable memento of the good days I spent in the bosom of that fine family, notwithstanding the smallpox.

The day after I got there, Dixon came to tell me that we were invited to a banquet in a neighboring wigwam, and that it was being given in honor of our arrival. I accepted the invitation and we went over there. Outside the wigwam we found a big fire with a large pot on it in which our banquet was cooking, and around the fire, seated on buffalo robes and deerskins were six Sioux warriors. We went from one to another shaking hands: then the pipe was lighted and passed several times around among the banqueters. Then everybody received an immense wooden plate containing 6 or 7 pounds of dried buffalo meat, and we began to eat. During my life I have seen some very big eaters, but none of them could have given me any idea of the voraciousness with which Indians can swallow gigantic portions. I was still at my fourth or fifth mouthful when they had already emptied their plates, and when I expressed astonishment the half-breed told me that that was nothing, that sometimes at scalping-parties they went from one wigwam to another and during a day would consume 5 or 6 platefuls like those (and without bursting). After we had eaten, the pipe was circulated and the Indians began to brag of their warlike exploits, and when we had listened to as much as politeness required, we went back to our own wigwam. The same day the chief of the tribe sent to ask us to a fresh-meat banquet. The half-breed, when he brought me the invitation, said, "White people sometimes have their ideas; so I must tell you one thing." I said, "As for me, I have no ideas at all, but tell me just the same." "Well," he said, "this is dog we are going to eat." "Good enough!" I said, "Let's have the dog. Come along." Just as at the other banquet, we found the chief with the most important warriors of the tribe sitting on the ground: same handshaking, same pipe-smoking as usual; then they served the dinner. It was a big young dog that formed the principal dish. I don't know whether it was because I had gone a long while without eating fresh meat, or whether dog-meat really is good, but the fact is that I found it perfect. The taste is like a fairly old calf and just a trifle leathery. When we had finished it they served us the broth, which I found bitter and bad. Then they passed around an empty plate to gather up the bones, so as to burn them and throw the ashes into the river, a ceremony always observed at a dog-feast, because that is a *medicine* feast, or in other words religious. After the meal, again the pipes, and again the speeches, always on the topic of their feats of arms, and I am too discreet to repeat them literally.

Dixon had led me to hope that he would make the entire trip with me, but when he now found himself in the bosom of his family, which at this critical juncture felt need of the protection of its head, he procured me a Canadian hunter and a Sioux guide who was expected from one moment to the next, and whose name in the tribe was *Eagle*; for the savages are not yet so far advanced in genealogical science as to have family names, but each individual has a name given him either because of some physical or moral characteristic or because of some chance occurrence.

Finally, after being awaited three days, Eagle arrived. I got ready to travel, and on the 25 August in the morning I started out for the St. Pierre River and the Falls of St. Anthony, with an escort of two men and four horses; and under the protection of two such brave saints I hoped to reach my destination without any serious accident.

Before my departure I was present at a curious ceremony, that of piercing, or really rather of cutting, a baby's ears. The savage who has the honor of performing this operation begins by making a very lengthy speech, in which he recounts all his own deeds of valor. After that, with his knife he slashes the ears of the unhappy child, which doesn't even heave a sigh.

Thereupon the father made a present of a horse to the ear-cutter, who ran about the whole camp for an hour or two, cracking his throat to shout the praises of the man who gave him the horse, and advertising that act of generosity.

The afternoon of the day before my departure I was invited to a feast. The ceremonies were the same as usual, but the feast this time was vegetarian. When hunting is poor the Indian lives on roots. The commonest variety they call a *pomme blanche.** It is a kind of woodeny turnip, which when raw has a taste between a turnip and a mushroom. The root is crushed, then it is boiled in buffalo fat—it is very good. As neither I nor the half-breed was able to consume a whole portion, we were obliged to carry what was left home, a custom always observed in such a case.

The Sioux lodges are made of buffalo or deer hide and in a conical shape. Their diameter is about 12 feet, and their height 15 or 16. They are supported by poles stuck into the ground in a circle and tightly tied together above. The buffalo skins well sewn together, are stretched in such a way as to leave a hole for smoke at the top. There is another small opening below, to enter by, which can be closed. Ordinarily these dwellings serve as lodgings for some twenty persons.

The evening before I left there was a dance. The only music was a few singers who accompanied themselves by tapping with a piece of wood. At the start the dance was a sort of *adagio,*

* Chittenden says (p. 806), "The Indian turnip or *pomme blanche* of the French (psoralea esculenta)." And on the next page, "It was a nutritious food and extensively used."

merely poses, grotesque and rather ugly. Then, so to speak, came the *allegro* which went in a *crescendo*. You would have said that the devil had entered into their bodies. Their feet, legs, hands and arms, their whole bodies moved in the most infernal and scarcely imaginable manner. Their singular music is very monotonous and made up of only two or three notes at most. Ordinarily it is in the minor, with no other modulations than that of emitting the sounds with more force or with less. At times it reminded me of priests in Italian villages who on very solemn feast-days put more than their usual rabidity into tearing God's ears and those of the faithful.

VI

To la Framboise with Eagle for Guide.

When Heaven was ready, I left the Missouri and the Vermilion or White Stone River, with my Sioux, Eagle, and a Canadian *free trapper** named Auguste. The Sioux wore his native costume: that is to say, his stiff black hair hung down on his shoulders; a very bright-colored calico handkerchief was knotted about his head; a short shirt, which was also of bright calico, covered him down to the hips; his foot-gear was moccasins, a kind of slipper made of buffalo hide and embroidered with porcupine quills; and for modesty he wore what the Canadians call a flap, which is nothing more than a piece of cloth or leather that passes between the legs and is fastened before and behind to a belt tight around the hips. From that belt my Sioux had hung a scalping-knife, a tobacco-pouch, a pipe, a small mirror to help him in painting his face and arranging feathers on his head, and a

* In English in the text.

fan or fly-chaser made of a hawk's wing. Finally, as a finishing touch, over all this he wore a buffalo robe, caught in at the waist and falling over his horse. His weapons were a musket, a bow and arrows, and his *tomahawk* or head-breaker, which after all is nothing but a hatchet. Eagle also had a leather sack for bullets fastened round his neck and hanging on his chest, and a powder-box made of a buffalo's horn. All in all he was a fine-looking man of about 40, tall, spare, with well-developed muscles, a good frank expression, although a little (or even a great deal) hard and ferocious, especially when he painted himself red around the eyes. He had two little stars tattooed one on his forehead, the other on his chin, and four lines on his cheeks. Eagle rode a good little wild horse, well-made and a very swift runner. A quarter of an hour after our departure the savage began a song of departure, which is not the one for which you go to Ste. Pélagie* and if I hadn't had a sample of Sioux music the night before, I should have thought my guide was going mad or was

* *"Le Chant du départ,"* only less popular as a Revolutionary song than the *"Marseillaise,"* though officially dropped by Napoleon, was dear to him, and was played in the theatres during the *Cent Jours*. Arese knew or assumed that the singing of it under Louis Philippe would suffice to send a person to the political prison of Ste. Pélagie.

taken with cholera. The savages have several songs that they call by bizarre names: for instance, the song of the bull, of the eagle, the bear, of death, war, departure, arrival. It is not that a given song sings the praises of the bull or the bear, or that there is any imitation of the noises they make, but simply that one melody (since they call such howlings melody) is dedicated to the merits of a certain animal or event. Generally their songs have no words; and those that have are made up of only 4 or 5 repeated over and over, as, for instance: "I arrive, open the door for me, open, open, open, open the door for me, open the door for I arrive," and so on until the voice gives out. They have no poetry, and rarely even jingle.

When our days went by without accident, they were all much alike. We were on horseback before sunrise. During the morning we tried to kill something for dinner: usually ducks, herons, bustards. If the horses were not too tired, or we were lucky, we chased a deer. We went on till about 11 o'clock A. M.; then we dismounted, cut a little grass, so as not (involuntarily) to set the prairie on fire, took the horses to drink, got water from the river, picked up or burned down some wood, lighted a fire, plucked ducks or skinned our larger game, and made haste to cook our meal and eat it. All that was generally accomplished in an hour: when a man is hungry he works rapidly. A half-hour later we remounted and rode until about 5 o'clock P. M. All the morning chores were done by me and the Canadian, for the savages have the bad habit of never doing anything. Eagle limited himself to unsaddling his horse and lighting a bit of straw to start the fire; then he smoked his pipe, wrapped himself in his buffalo robe, and slept until the meal was served. In the evening, when we had halted and the savage had lighted the fire and smoked his pipe, he took his weapons and went to make a round to see that we had no undesirable neighbors. An hour later he got back for dinner, and what is strange is that he always brought something to eat, either plums, or grapes (whose memory sets my teeth on edge), or hazel-nuts, or onions, or *pommes blanches*, or I don't remember what else. When he found some, he never failed to bring back *canicanick,** a kind of wood that one scrapes and mixes with tobacco to form a very good smoking mixture.

* Chittenden says (p. 808), "Kinikinik . . . consisted of the leaves or inner bark of certain shrubs. Among those were the leaves of the smooth sumac (Rhus Glabra); the inner bark of the red-osier dogwood or so-called red willow (Cornus Stolenifera) and the leaves and bark of the bear berry (Arctostaphylos uva ursi)."

After dinner we all three made rounds in different directions, and if everything was perfectly quiet we let the horses roam where they would. Then we smoked several pipes and then wrapped up warmly in our coats and covers and slept till morning, provided the animals in the forest and the insects, were willing.

An hour before day we roused the fire, to warm and dry ourselves, went to find the horses, and then off with us!

That is about the way our trip went. But besides that, almost every day there were slight scares or accidents, which are not worth writing down. They were all much alike.

I went along the Sioux River to the River des Rochers,* always across the prairies. But as these were higher than the ones I had crossed on my first trip, they were also more beautiful, and above all, easier to travel over. They were drier, and not the sort that are called thereabouts cows' bellies or moving ground, that is to say, ground that gives, but without your sinking into it. The rivers are fine ones, with splendid sand bottoms, and just the necessary amount of water, and no more.

Once during this trip there was difficulty be-

* The Sioux is the boundary between Iowa and South Dakota. The Rock River empties into it in Sioux County, Iowa.

cause of a devilish little swamp where there was more water than I liked and no wood to make a float. I was in the mischief of a fix. I thought of all my friends, who had constantly preached to me to learn swimming, and I saw that they were right; but meanwhile my reflections weren't helping me to get to the other shore. Finally, after having called loudly on heaven and earth to assist me, I took all my courage in two hands and my horse's tail also, clinging to it as to a safety anchor; I drove him into the water, and flattering myself that I was swimming with my legs, in a few minutes I found that I was on the other bank. Hating water as I do, I confess that after that exploit I was pleased with myself, and when I looked back at the swamp I had just crossed* in such a curious manner, I felt that I had outdone myself. That great event happened the fourth or fifth day of our trip.

On the second day we had met a lodge of travelling Sioux—I mean a whole family party. We halted, of course we all shook hands and passed pipes around, and after a long conference be-

* Surely Arese refers to Dante's Inferno, I. 22-24:

> "And as a man who, winded with his pains
> To struggle from the ocean to the shore,
> Looks back to view the perilous watery plains:"

tween Eagle and the new friends we had just met, our guide told me—the Canadian interpreting, for he knew a few words of Sioux—that there were buffalo on the Red Pipe Stone River* and that if I chose I could hunt them without much lengthening our trip. — "Certainly. Let's go there," was my reply. So we turned back a little way up the Rock River, a pretty little stream that takes its name from the rocks running along part of its banks, rocks whose color is a greyish red.

It was a real pleasure for me, after so much prairie, to see rocks again. We found buffalo tracks, and pretty soon some way off we saw buffaloes, which appeared all one dark mass. We followed them for two days, going north along the Red Pipe Stone River. On the third day we lost all hope of overtaking them, because our horses were worn out and we were to windward and so could not surprise them without making a long detour. So we left them to their fate and turned our course south-east passing between the lakes that are at the source of the River Des Moines. These little lakes are very pretty, situated in the midst of prairies and bordered by woods of gigantic trees. On reaching the top of one of those rises that one frequently finds in the rolling

*Red Pipestone Creek in Pipestone County, Minnesota.

prairies, we saw something black in the distance. At first we thought it was our buffaloes and were already having a celebration about chasing them; but on getting closer we clearly made out three large Indian tents. We at once halted, looked to the saddle-girths, changed our primings, got our guns ready—in short prepared to defend ourselves or to flee (what a vile word!). The Canadian and I were soon ready, but not the Indian. He had stuck an arrow into the ground, hung his mirror on it, and was busy painting his face red and black and putting feathers on his head: that is, he was completing a toilet for presenting himself worthily to the enemy—a thing an Indian never fails to do. We started on again on foot leading our horses, so as to be hidden by the tall grass. We approached with great precautions—but unnecessarily. A very sad spectacle awaited us. When we arrived in front of a wigwam, a cloud of crows and birds of prey, and a few wolves, came out of it. These were the wigwams of the unlucky Sioux who had decamped when the smallpox began to rage at Vermilion; but the disease had followed them, and we found nothing left of them but what the wolves and the birds of prey had not yet eaten. We saw men's bones and horses' mixed together, a few remnants of clothes and weapons. It was horrible and at the same time disgusting. We left this frightful spectacle as soon as possible, and all the rest of that day we met wolves.

In order not to lose time while we still hoped to catch up with the buffalo, we had neglected to shoot anything, and while counting on a good dinner we had used up all our provisions. When we turned back on our path again, we found no game: everything had probably fled in fright out of the way of the buffaloes; and for nearly 48 hours we went without anything's passing our teeth, excepting a few quids of tobacco, and that's not very nourishing. At the end of the second day of fasting we camped on the shore of a little lake, which was covered with ducks. We all three got down on our stomachs so as not to frighten the game, and keeping alongside the lake we began to shoot. It was like a first-line rattle of musketry. At the end of a short half-hour we had 19 ducks. We hastened to light a fire, but the kettle would hold only six. Those six we ate before they were cooked much. A second batch quickly followed the first; and prudence alone prevented us from adding a third edition of six more ducks. Unluckily our hunger was so violent that it made us forget to hitch our horses. After supper it was already dark. The Canadian went to look for them, and half an hour later he came back saying he had not found them. We thought they had been stolen. The region we were in was not one to inspire much confidence. So the savage got his weapons ready and started off with the Canadian. I remained alone to guard the camp, and I took every precaution: I carefully lowered the fire, but left enough to serve as a rallying-point for my two men, and not enough to let any one see how many people there were in camp, supposing somebody came to attack us. Around the fire I placed four bundles of grass inside our blankets and buffalo robes, as if four men were sleeping around the fire. As always, I examined my weapons to see that they were in order; and after lighting a pipe I lay down in the grass some twenty paces away from the fire on the shore of the lake, so that I might see anybody arrive without being seen myself.

Luckily all this was superfluous. Two hours later the two men returned with the horses, and we digested the twelve ducks at our ease. The day preceding we had already had one false alarm: we were sitting around the fire smoking our pipes, which alas! took the place of dinner, when all at once we heard horses come galloping toward us. That very instant we were on our feet, or rather we were crouching in the grass, our guns in our hands, waiting the attack. And it was only our own horses bearing down swiftly upon us. The Indian told us that it was a bad sign, that the horses had smelt Indians and it would be prudent to move—which we did.

Wild horses' instincts are truly marvellous—they very often announce an enemy's arrival to their masters, and when they have been stolen, they very often escape from their new owners to return to their old ones, even at hundreds of miles away. Those poor beasts have a special talent for recognizing marshy soil; they tap with one hoof without bearing weight on it before they will venture, and I well remember once when my poor horse didn't wish to enter a river. I wanted to cross, and I forced him to. In the middle of the current I had to dismount in the water because my horse was bemired up to his belly, and I had to get a pole to dislodge him with. After that, whenever my horse resisted at the brink of a stream, I left the reins loose on his neck and went across at his side.

One time while travelling in the prairie along a rise of ground where the grass was about 6 feet high and where there were a lot of trees fallen down in it, my horse with his single eye, for the poor animal had but one, saw them at once and avoided them, whereas I in his place, even with my two eyes, should have broken my legs.

I shan't mention a lot of other little alarms and the precautions they caused us to take, for such was our life at every moment and those incidents are too trifling to report.

The ninth day we reached la Framboise,* a place that takes its name from a half-breed who lives and trades there. Two Indians came to meet us, and after exchanging two words with Eagle, shook hands with me and the Canadian, and when they had smoked the pipe etiquette demands, went back at a dead gallop. The Canadian said, "It's good that they're going back to the camp to say that the white men have arrived. Everybody will daub his face and they'll put the kettle on."

We were entering the wood that surrounds the

* Bishop A. Ravoux in his "Reminiscences." St. Paul, 1890, says "Laframboise at Little Rock on the Minnesota River." That was in 1841. Little Rock is or was five miles below Fort Ridgeley in Nicollet County. ("Minnesota in Three Centuries," New York, 1908, II, 326.) Nicollet says (p. 13), "Mr. J. Laframboise . . . to whom I am indebted for much valuable information obtained during my campaign of 1838, lived there for several years." He is speaking of the "Great Oasis," between Lakes Sarah and Shatek in Murray County. He says the Des Moines River rose there: and we have seen a few pages back that Arese was precisely there when he first saw the buffalo. So perhaps Laframboise had moved to Little Rock by 1837.

small lake on whose shores M. la Framboise's shack is situated, when we met two savages on horseback. The elder of them spoke to Eagle, who on answering, offered his hand. The old man refused to take it. The Canadian coming close to me, said, "That's not a good sign. Things aren't going so well as I expected. In any case, let's be ready to shoot first." He made use of all his knowledge and succeeded in discovering that the trouble was on account of the smallpox, that the old man, the chief of the tribe, was afraid we might be bringing that disease among them from the Sioux. After a long discussion the chief, who had only one arm, went ahead with his companion and we followed them to M. la Framboise's house. That house consisted of two rooms built of tree trunks and mud. One room is kitchen and bedroom, the other is the store. Two months before la Framboise had gone away and left his house to a Canadian who had been living there with him. He received us most cordially. I slept there and he furnished me with a number of things I needed —powder, shot, tobacco, cornmeal, and salt which I had felt the lack of for some while—that is, since my pack-horse had got mired in the river. When I wished to pay for my board and my men's, he refused to let me, saying that he was the one that ought to pay because of the great pleasure my visit had given him. "Just think," he added, "during the ten years I've been here, you are the second white man I've seen." He begged me to stay and rest a day longer, but I had lost too much time over those rascally buffaloes, and by 5 the next morning I was in the saddle.

My host, who spoke Sioux like a Sioux, was kind enough to serve as interpreter between me and the old chief who came to call on me and invited me to go see him in his tent, where I spent a most agreeable and interesting evening. The old one-armed lad, whose name meant Running Cloud or Storm, was chief of the famous band called the Five Wigwams. He begged my pardon for not having shaken hands that morning, explained that it was out of fear of the disease and not through lack of the respect one owes to a great man, as he called all Europeans or Englishmen—which for the Indians comes to the same thing.

Duncas, the Canadian I was stopping with, had told me the story of Running Cloud. He himself repeated it to me. Here it is:

At the time of the last war between the Americans and the English, the savages in general were on the side of the latter. Running Cloud was no mere warrior in his tribe: on account of his courage and cleverness he had been elected chief of the so-called band of the Five Wigwams, for although that tribe grew later until it counted 600 fighting-men, it was then made up of only 5 wigwams.

Running Cloud counts among his exploits that of the Battle of Mackinaw, in which with 90 men he forced 800 Americans to take to their boats, and he also claimed the taking of the fort at Prairie du Chien. The commander of the English army that wanted to attack the fort, told Running Cloud to wait until he himself had summoned the place to surrender, ordering him to camp near the fortress and await orders. Before daybreak the English commander marched toward Running Cloud's camp, but found it empty. He pushed on toward the fort, and heard firing from afar. Running Cloud took the fort and the English captain arrived just in time to stop the butchery. After these and various other deeds of valor the English gave him a medal and a flag, which he is extremely proud of. They also gave him a pension, which he has never taken, saying that he was always pleased to leave his family and fight for his masters against the *Long Knives* (a name the Indians honor the Americans with), but not pleased to be paid for it. The war being over, his band turned its courage from the path of honor and followed that of murder, robbery, and pillage, and made itself terrible even among the Sioux and the other tribes. Running Cloud did everything he could to make his men behave themselves, but in vain. He had no desire to be the chief of a gang that dishonored him, and from then on he never exercised his authority except to prevent some crime. One time a warrior of his tribe wanted to assassinate a white man: the old chief used all his eloquence to dissuade him, and finished his harangue by saying, "If it is the thirst for gore that is devouring you, *kill me*; but do not stain your hands with the blood of those who have been so good to us. In any case you will have to pass over my body to reach him." Scarcely had Running Cloud turned around before the Indian planted a bullet in his back which came out through his chest. The bystanders seized him, they wanted to put the murderer to death. But Running Cloud prevented that, saying that his own order had been obeyed. His family and friends expected him to die after such a wound. They started their weeping and the funeral chants; but the old chief had other ideas. He remembered that when hunting he had often sent a ball right through a buffalo, which had not died; and he reflected: "An Indian is about the same as a buffalo, and I don't see for what reason I should die." He sang the song of the buffalo, left his bed, and crawled on hands and knees into the prairie, looking for herbs whose juice would be efficacious. He showed me where the bullet had passed, where it had gone in and where come out; also many other wounds his body was riddled with. It really is astonishing that after such a number of them he could not only live but even enjoy good health. Some time later the warriors of his band stole horses belonging (I think) to the Government. Running Cloud was put in prison, although he had had no part in the robbery. Cynical tongues say that revenge had something to do with his imprisonment, since sometimes even Governments or those representing them, are so vile as to take vengeance on a single individual, and that the American Government—like many others in this—seized the chance to revenge itself for defeats that the Indian had played so leading a rôle in inflicting. Running Cloud tried to escape from the fort where he was imprisoned, and a bullet the sentinel shot at him broke his arm and one of his ribs. Finally the horses were given back and the savage was restored to liberty.—Though he has only one arm, he is an excellent hunter and very skilful at carving pipes from red clay. I desired to buy a very nicely decorated one, but he told me he didn't care to sell it and had refused a fine horse for it. Since I was not disposed to offer him a team, I let it go, and he made me a present of his own pipe, apologizing for not being able to give me a better one. I asked Duncas why the chief did not care to sell the other pipe, and he told me that the Indians thereabouts attached considerable importance to it because it represents two heads, something after the manner of a Janus, and that when there was some quarrel among them, the old man made them all smoke this pipe and that reconciled them. I asked him if he still liked war. He answered, "If the masters of Europe need me again, worthless as I am, I will take my gun and my arrows," he said, "in hand once more. But as for making war on our nations who are already enough tormented by the white men—never! Those who go to war all find the paths closed or filled with thorns, but I am free and can go where I choose. My son, who is a handsome lad, has several times asked me to let him go to war. I've always prevented it, and if he tells me enemies are coming, I reply, 'String your bow, get the flint ready in your gun, and wait for them firmly at your own wigwam.' I should weep with joy," he added, "if my son were killed defending his wigwam, whereas I should be very unhappy, if he brought back a scalp he had gone to look for in the enemies' camp."

This Indian, like all of them no matter what tribe they belong to, expressed contempt and irreconcilable hatred for the Americans, and loved Europeans, French or English without distinction. He told me: "According to what I have heard, in your country when a powerful man" (a Government) "makes a man miserable unjustly, as the Americans made me, he tries to lessen the wrong he has done. But Americans are like pigs, which think of nothing but filling their bellies, and they do that at our expense." Although little convinced of the correctness of his ideas, I took care not to undeceive him. I asked him if it was long since he had travelled. He replied: "Since my treasure has been buried here" (he referred to a beloved daughter who was dead) "I have never left this place, and I never shall leave it except to get nearer to my dear child." When I arrived to call on Running Cloud, I had found him sitting in front of his tent holding a piece of red stone between his feet and working it with his one hand. He was surrounded by 4 children and his two wives. For this fine man permits himself the enjoyment of two of them. He gave me hominy to eat, made me the present of a pipe that pleased me greatly, and it was very late in the evening when I quitted him to go home to bed. Before bidding me good-bye he gave me the sage advice to fasten my horses well and to be on the alert, because the region was not a safe one.

During the day I saw at the trading station one of the prettiest red-skin women I have ever come across. She resembled, if I am permitted to make the comparison, a very pretty young Russian lady I once met in Switzerland. She was well made, had beautiful eyes, a beautiful mouth, and most beautiful teeth. Her color, like that of the Northern Indians, was not very dark—rather olive than red. Her husband was a hunter. I was lucky enough to give him a pound of powder and two of shot to kill me ducks with, and the splendid fellow went off and returned two hours later bringing me eight ducks. They were excellent. I never ate such good ones!

[VII]

To Traverse des Sioux & by Canoe to the Mouth.

THE next day we left, early in the morning; and toward noon the Indian set the prairie behind us on fire,—a fine idea: it wiped out our traces and might also help to retard the advance of any one who coveted our horses, which were no longer able to go very well, so much had the pursuit of the buffaloes and some few deer worn them out, to say nothing of the excessive August heat, the forced marches, and the mosquitoes, which ate them up and made them bleed as if they had been pricked with a lancet. The poor beasts were as thin as swallows, and I still had some days' going ahead of me before reaching Traverse des Sioux,* and from there three more to get to the Mississippi, and these last three through the trembling swamp land. If I had acted prudently, I should have waited some days longer, to rest our mounts; but I did otherwise: I

* Traverse des Sioux was in what is now Nicollet County, Minnesota. Its P. O. address is St. Peter.

decided to give two of the horses with the saddles, buffalo robes, kettles, all my travelling kit, to the two men as payment; and the third horse I wanted to exchange for a canoe which could take me from Traverse des Sioux to the place where the St. Pierre River flows into the Mississippi. During the last days of our land-trip game was more abundant than ever, and among our delicacies I must count a turtle, which was excellent even though we cooked him without salt, without pepper, without any sort of seasoning, simply in his own natural juice. One thing that astonished me was the vitality of the animal. We fished him in the morning toward 8 o'clock, smashed his head flat with the butt of a musket, so as to make it lose even its shape, then we put a slipknot around his neck, attached it to the saddle of a horse, and the wretched turtle trotted and galloped until evening. Then he was loosened from the horse; but when we began cutting off his shell, the poor beast was still alive, for he reached out his claws—but in vain: the cauldron awaited him.

In those last days of the trip we saw a black bear, which ran away as we drew near.

I passed between the two Swan Lakes,* which

* They are in Nicollet County, Minnesota.

are very pretty ones, surrounded by trees. One of them is of nice clear water. In the prairie and the woods you very seldom see all those little birds that enliven the scene, which you see masses of in Europe. In this country the smallest birds are the starling, which is black and red, and the swallow. I have frequently remarked the swallows flying round about the horses and following us for leagues at a time, as if to make a festa for travellers that risked themselves in such deserts; and in my sentimental reveries I took pleasure in seeing in them the memories of some good friend, who, I thought, must be thinking of me at that moment.* This is an idea that revives your morale completely, especially when you have been entirely isolated for a long while. Another thing that gave me enormous joy was that the greater number of the objects of prime necessity I had with me, were gifts from friends, very intimate friends—my musket, my pistols, my knives, my pipe, etc., etc.: and every time I used them a thought of friendliness and gratitude went out to the persons I had received them from, as if to thank them for the good service their presents were doing me. And as this is not the first time I have undertaken this type of trip, on my departure I chose by prefer-

* The text here is obscure, but the meaning clear.

ence things that had been given me rather than those I had bought.

Before I left, among the many pieces of advice they gave me was one against wearing any chains or rings or carrying gold or anything else glittering,* which might arouse the cupidity of the Indians. I followed that advice: only I could not bring myself to leave off carrying a talisman given me by the Duchesse de St. Leu.† She pre-

* Arese's word is "chisquant," which may be a misprint for clinquant, or possibly one invented by him with some Italian word in mind.

† When his brother Louis had abdicated the throne of Holland, Napoleon settled a property called St. Leu on the ex-Queen Hortense. At the first Bourbon restoration the government allowed her the title of Duchesse de St. Leu; and though all the steps necessary to make that title official were never taken, Hortense was widely known by it. What she thought about the talisman may be gathered from what she wrote in her memoirs. ("Mémoires de la Reine Hortense," Paris: 1927, vol. II, p. 22). In 1808 she says: "It was the fashion at that time to collect precious stones engraved by the Turks, and I had a great quantity of them. I imagined that a seal presented by me might serve as a talisman, or at least I found pleasure in making myself think so, in order that by being able to distribute little souvenirs to many people I might be able to send one to one person, and besides I liked to tell myself: why should not I too have some compensation? If my lot is unhappy, at least let me bring happiness to others; then I shall no longer dare to complain about destiny. So I gave all the Emperor's aides-de-camp and other officers seals which I advised them to be sure to carry if they wished to be saved from danger. . . . In reality it happened that almost all of those who had my talismans did escape from every peril. . . . General Colbert lost his during a battle; he begged me

sented it to me on my departure for Africa, saying that it would bring me luck and protect me from danger. So whenever something fortunate for me occurred, and especially when I had escaped some danger, I attributed it all to the talisman; and every night on winding my watch, when the talisman brushed against my hand I always thought with respectful affection and veneration of Her whom I love as I love my mother, and who has always heaped kindnesses upon me. And besides it was impossible for me to stop wearing a turquoise ring that my mother had given me six years before, when, leaving my native land I had left her too. Several times I noticed that the ring attracted the Indians' attention; but that did not disturb me: the pistols I carried in my belt were a good sedative for their desires.

It seems to me that, when I began speaking of my friends, I started in to be pathetic. Well, when a decent man has been three months hearing nothing talked about except war-trails, robbery, rapine, massacres, scalps, or at the least

to send him another. I was about to do so when I learned of his death. . . . I discovered that I had changed what was originally a joke into a superstition, for afterwards I never failed to send one to my brother for every campaign, and I should have been worried if he had not carried it." Some years later (vol. II, p. 273) she tells of giving one to Ypsilanti bound for Greece.

grizzly bears, buffaloes, beavers, etc., etc., he may well be permitted to indulge in a bit of sentiment, especially when he does so in private and in writing. One can scarcely imagine the singular effect produced on a rather active imagination by two or three months of silence, especially when a lot of unusual objects are continually startling him. The silence I was condemned to was not absolute, since I could use signs with my Indian and chatter with my Canadian: but a conversation in pantomime does not get very far, and as for my Canadian, after three days' riding, I knew all his ideas by heart. So then I came to passing whole days in reveries; and toward evening my imagination was so worn out and my thoughts so confused that I realized that that is how people go crazy.

In these last days of the trip I have seen rats of a curious species. They are land rats that have two little bags of skin outside the muzzle and the neck, which they fill with earth during their underground work, and then come out to empty. They are greyish in hue and larger than land rats ordinarily are.*

Day before yesterday I had a discussion with my

*Some species of gopher. See "U. S. War Department Reports of Exploration and Surveys," Washington, 1857. Vol. VIII, under "Gopher."

Sioux, which although confined entirely to signs, was nevertheless rather lively: and this is why: as it is pretty fatiguing to lead the file, the lazy savage—lazy like all those of his race—was usually avoiding going on ahead and usually I was the one to do it. That day I had led the way all morning; but after dinner I felt tired and told the Sioux to go first. He had to be urged, and then started; but instead of going at a traveller's trot (which is to say, an amble) he went very slowly. I asked him once to go faster and he answered that I had better take the lead. I told him a second time; and as I had no greater success, I ordered him to halt. I repeated that he was to go ahead, and if he did not, he would be sorry: and as I said that I slipped two balls into the barrels of my musket, made it ready, and let it lie across my horse's neck. Fortunately he made off at a fast trot and went along very well the whole day. I say fortunately, because if he had not obeyed, or if he had made the slightest grimace, I was quite ready to sweep him off his horse. I may even add that if I had been in front of him instead of behind, I should not have had so much patience but after having spoken to him once, my gun should have had the job of speaking the second time. But I could not bring myself to shooting him in the back, though that is the Indian habit. That evening when we reached our halting-place, the Canadian told me I had done a very good thing in making him understand reason; but he advised me to be on my guard that night, and said he should be too. Although Eagle after dinner had handed me his pipe to puff at, I stayed awake until my companions were asleep, and then I took the Indian's musket and emptied the powder out from the pan, on which I dropped a few drops of saliva. I lighted a fire, I strolled about, I smoked, I chewed tobacco, till worn out, but it was quite impossible for me to manage to keep my eyes open; and when I saw that sleep was winning against fear—or rather, against the instinct of self-preservation—I made my weapons ready, and with my hands on the handles of my pistols I slept tranquilly until morning.

The next day toward noon we found many tracks, and the Indian, according to his custom, dismounted and for a long while traced them ahead and back. He made his examination with great care, as if he had been ordered to draw up an official report; and he came back with a long face to inform me that a strong war-party had passed there not over an hour before, and that we must positively turn our horses in another direction and ride as hard as we could. Luckily we were already across the St. Pierre River, which had caused us some trouble. We rode as fast as our horses' strength allowed, and arrived three hours later at Traverse des Sioux. On learning the route we had taken we were astonished to find ourselves arriving there.* We learned that the tracks we had seen were those of a war-party of Sacs and Foxes, 150 warriors strong. It had been a lucky thing for me to avoid it, particularly as I had a Sioux for guide. Without a doubt I should have lost my two dozen remaining hairs.

At Traverse des Sioux there is a small station of the American Fur Company, and there I traded my horse for a little boat. I made that bargain with two Indians. Then, leaving my two guides, I went down the River St. Pierre to where it falls into the Mississippi.

Before we said good-bye, I and my two guides reproached ourselves for having set fire to the prairie every evening for our diversion and the enjoyment of a fine spectacle, because it might have attracted the attention and the curiosity of our enemies' war-party: a curiosity that would

* That is what the text says; but I think Arese must have meant to write "they were astonished to see us arrive there." In French the difference would be only two words.

have been satisfied at our expense. But that didn't happen, and luckily it didn't!

It may have appeared amazing that my Indian was able to say positively that the tracks we had seen were not over an hour old. I myself, though accustomed to that sort of life for a long time and consequently used to examining everything with meticulous attention, since my life depended on it, must admit that I considered his assertion a bit rash. This is how he explained it: "When grass is pressed down when there is no dew on it, it stays down. Now you can see," he told me, "that this grass is lying down. That shows that somebody has passed over it since the dew evaporated; and as it is at most an hour that the sun has dried it . . . " The conclusion was legitimate. Besides, he showed me ashes knocked from pipes: it was dry, but the bottom of the tobacco was still moist.

Maybe somebody will say, how could you carry on such a long conversation, not knowing the Sioux language? I will reply first of all, that the Canadian knew some words of Sioux; next, that when you have passed some forty days with a person whom you have to make understand in regard to the prime necessities of existence, if that person is not lacking in intelligence* the matter

*Along with Wabasha and Little Crow there was one Eagle

is soon adjusted and the dictionary soon found.

One time I had an even more abstract conversation. I told my guide that I thought we were bearing too much toward the West. He was astonished at my remark, and admitting that it was true, that he had taken that direction in order to avoid some swamps and ponds that would have obliged us to go a long way round, he asked me if I had travelled through that region before. On my negative response, he questioned me. He asked me how I knew the district. Then I showed him a map, which he understood perfectly, and my compass, which aroused his enthusiasm and curiosity, and which he kept turning about this way and that way, trying to bring the magic needle to rest. At that time I was unable to make him understand anything more than that by means of that needle, which always kept its direction, one could always know approximately where one was. At the beginning of my trip, for fear that my guide might abandon me or might

in the conference of the Sioux chief with the governor of Minnesota Territory in 1853 or 4 ("Minnesota Historical Society Collections," Saint Paul, 1880," III, 320), and this may have been Arese's guide. No doubt it was, for Nicollet says in his "Report" (p. 45) that the chief of a party of Yankton [Sioux] Indians, "friends or connexions of Dixon," was the Eagle; "one of the most intelligent and brave Indians with whom" Nicollet "ever became acquainted." That was in 1839.

be killed, in order not to find myself in a sort of sea of prairies without any idea where to go, I took my precautions. I kept a kind of *log-book** as one does at sea. Mornings, before starting, I found where I was on my map by means of the sun and the compass; and in the evening, having again found my position, I marked how many leagues I had covered and in what direction. Accordingly, had an accident happened, I should always have known within some leagues where I was, and consequently what direction to take.

Several times, in the midst of prairies, and particularly of high prairies, I noticed a certain number of blocks of stone, generally granite, without being able to comprehend how they got there. Mountains were far away; the small rivers rise in the prairies themselves; and the Missouri and the Mississippi are too distant for me to assume that those great boulders could have been carried there by those streams. What made it even more extraordinary is that these granite blocks occur only in the high prairies and near the edges, that they are rounded in shape, and that they have a rather smooth and one might almost say pretty surface. I asked a good many people for the explanation of the phenomenon, but they all left

* In English in the text.

me in my pristine ignorance; and it was only afterwards that I learned that one must count those blocks among the number of what the geologists call the "erratic group."

I took three days to descend the St. Pierre River from Traverse des Sioux to the Mouth.*

The fine weather, which had been faithful to me until then, deserted me, and for a long while I had grievous weather.

The River St. Pierre is a pretty little stream which widens out to 80 rods. While descending it I had a storm magnificent as to thunder and lightning. It lasted all night. There were times when the whole sky was on fire and I could see as distinctly as by bright sunlight at noon. If this on the one hand was poetical, it had also its disastrous aspect. The rain fell in torrents all the night, and next morning I shot the Little Rapid, which is nothing more than a very small waterfall and reached the Mouth very safely, having met nothing but a considerable number of In-

* From "Minnesota in Three Centuries," New York, 1908, Vol. I, p. 138, we learn that in 1826 Faribault built a house at St. Peter's, now Mendota, and that Mendota was the Dakota word "meaning the mouth of a river," where the St. Pierre, now the Minnesota, empties into the Mississippi. Fort Snelling was built north of the smaller river, Mendota south of it, and later St. Paul east of the bigger one.

dian canoes ascending the river to go hunting. Among those canoes there was one of Canadian hunters on their way to Lake Traverse. They greeted my boat, and when they saw in me an individual they did not know, they asked me if I belonged to the Opposition. Half asleep, musing perhaps about politics, their question struck me as very strange. "The devil!" I said to myself; "They ought to pay no attention to anything but buffaloes and beavers. Why are they mixing into politics?" But the explanation is that among the hunters themselves there is an opposition. Whatever does not belong to the American Fur Company is called "Opposition" and the more ground the "Opposition" gains, the better it is for the hunters and the clerks of the American Fur Company, and even for the savages; for the former are better paid and the latter less robbed. The jealousy between the "American" and the "Opposition" goes at times perhaps too far and departs entirely from parliamentary rules. I have been told (and by an employee of the "American") that on one occasion detachments of the two rival powers were encamped side by side with their men, their horses, and their merchandise, both of them on their way to trade with the savages, and during the night all the horses of the

"Opposition" were found to have been arrowed! I was told of several other equally serious happenings that I prefer not to believe. Or if they really were true, I am convinced that they never took place by order, or even with the consent of the American Fur Company, whose honor and correctness are above suspicion.

On the left bank of the River St. Pierre and the right of the Mississippi, stands Fort Snelling,* which perhaps is a fortification against the Indians, but which I would not call a barracks for regular troops. It is built in a very fine position. On the opposite bank there is a post of the American Fur Company, which counts more men in its service than there are in the Federal fort.

The two days I remained there I occupied very usefully in going to see the falls of Little Falls' Creek,† a very small river not more than 20 feet wide at the spot where the falls are; and those are 30 odd feet high. The stream goes over a rock perfectly semicircular in form and hollow beneath, so that the water forms a very pretty and elegant veil. The falls are so beautiful and so regular that you would be inclined to call them a work of art rather than of nature. I also went to

* Now on the outskirts of St. Paul.

† The Little Falls and the creek are now called Minnehaha.

see the Falls of the Mississippi, called St. Anthony's. They are only 2 leagues below where the Mississippi begins to be navigable by small steamboats and then during only certain months of the year. The falls are about 30 feet high and 360 rods in breadth. Their shape is fairly regular and resembles three semicircles, the two smaller of which are on the two sides of the large one, whose form is very much that of a horse-shoe. The three semicircles are separated each from each by a pile of boulders and tree trunks brought down by the current. Opposite the central circle there is a very singular rock which aims the likeness of a vessel's prow toward the falls. The banks of the Mississippi are covered with fine firs and cedars.

I went to see the Indian tribe called *Black Dogs.** I found them having a festival dance. One of their war parties had brought home two scalps of Sacs, who are an enemy tribe. This gave me a chance to witness their war-dance. Men and women formed a large ring around the scalps stretched on poles and smoothed out on two frames which they were tied to with string, like skins on a drum or canvas on an embroidery-frame. Everybody jumped around the circle either with both feet side by side or on one leg

* English in the original.

with the other held in the air, yelling and howling like mad wolves. I tried to imitate their song, and for days afterwards my throat was scraped to pieces—and that without having succeeded. They were painted and dressed for the ceremony as if for war, and I found them more hideous than ever.

As I had spoken to the clerk of the American Fur Company on my arrival about the party of Sacs and Foxes that was prowling about near the River St. Pierre, the report spread, and the next day there was a heap of Indians to learn details about numbers and the place where I had seen the tracks.

I went to see Lake Calhoun and Lake Harriet, which are not very far away from the Mouth and which are very pretty little lakes. I also visited the village of Cold Water,* so named from a spring flowing across it.

* Cold Water was very near Fort Snelling. Cf. William Watts Folwell, "A History of Minnesota," Saint Paul, Vol. I, 1921, p. 137, footnote 19.

VIII

Down the Mississippi in a Dug-out to Prairie du Chien.

Two days after my arrival at the Mouth, I left there in a dug-out with two Canadians to go down the Mississippi as far as Prairie du Chien. The sight of the Mississippi gave me great pleasure; it was as if I met an old acquaintance, and one who had grown younger and prettier; for this was not the immensely broad river with flat banks and muddy water that I had left at Saint Louis, but a pretty stream of nice fair dimensions sweeping along in clear waves and having on its shores fine rocks crowned with evergreens and sweet hills carpeted with agreeable green. Some leagues from the Mouth there is a cave on the left bank that has some reputation in that region; but on comparing it to those in Virginia, I could not keep from exclaiming, "Oh, what rubbish!"

I went through the Indian village of the Little Crows,* where I traded flour and salt pork for

* He means, of course, Little Crow, the celebrated chief of that name. It was called Kaposia.

venison. I crossed Lake St. Croix,* which is 12 miles long and 3 wide, and into which empties the river of the same name. I went by the village of Aigle Rouge† and that of Tour des Pins,‡ and I reached Lake Pepin. Vile little lake, which made me lose so much time and gain so much rain! During the whole voyage I had the wind against me, so that I took 7 days instead of 3. Only the

*It is hard to see why Arese should have crossed it unless he went out of his way to do so; for it was not on the route from the mouth of the St. Pierre to Prairie du Chien. But it was not far out of the way, and he may have been curious about it. Or might he have mistaken Spring Lake for it? Hardly. But the official map of the Mississippi River Commission calls the St. Croix at the point where it empties into the Mississippi "Lake St. Croix." So perhaps Arese meant merely that he crossed the mouth of it.

†The text here has "l'Aile-Toge," though a little farther on it has "l'Aigle rouge." A compromise would give "l'Aile rouge," and the village of Red Wing is still in Goodhue County, Minnesota, near the head of Lake Pepin.

‡Major Stephen H. Long in his "Voyage in a Six-oared Skiff to the Falls of Saint Anthony in 1817," ("Minn. Hist. Soc. Coll." II, 29-30), says he "passed the Detour du Pin or Pine Turn of the Mississippi, which is the most westwardly turn of the river, between St. Louis and the Falls of St. Anthony." Arese may have been right in putting a village there twenty years later. Indian villages were movable. Today, however, Pine Bend, Dakota County, Minnesota, has no population (according to Rand, McNally), and its post-office address is Rich Valley. But those interested may compare Warren Upham, "Minnesota Geographic Names," Saint Paul, 1920, p. 167, under Pine Bend.

first day did I have fair weather, but during the night it started to rain and continued for nearly the whole trip.

In the afternoon of the second day I got to Lake Pepin, which is a rather pretty one, 7 leagues long and 3 wide. Despite its being so small it is dangerous enough to make steamboats stop. That day it rained and blew hard. I kept along shore, and then the two Canadians said that since we had to double a cape called Pointe au Sable* and to go out into open water, we must wait until the wind dropped; that usually the lake grew calm at evening. So we pulled our canoe on shore and patiently waited for evening in a beating rain. My canoe was a wooden one made of a tree trunk. It was 30 or 35 feet long and from ½ to 2 broad. When I was sitting on the bottom of it with my cape over me, I had a hard time moving, for the great trouble with such canoes is that they are very unsteady and a fairly heavy wave fills them at once. A person not accustomed to them hardly dares to move; but in a short while you learn to turn in every direction without making them lose their balance. One of my two Canadians called

* So A. spells it. The modern version is Point au Sable. Almost all voyagers on the lake in little boats agree about the vile weather frequent there.

Gamelle, was really no good except at mess,* and for nothing else. He was a coward, afraid of water, of wind, of the lake, the shots we could hear in the woods, and even, I believe, of the devil. He loathed work, but to balance that he loved sleeping. The other, on the contrary, named Tatan, rowed like one possessed, was always ready to go ahead. Finally evening came, but the wind did not appear to be dropping much. For an hour Gamelle had been pointedly recounting all the accidents that had ever taken place on Lake Pepin, and I believe in other places too, since the discovery of America, but without affecting me. But when I said: "Come on, children, the weather is pretty calm. Let's get on our way before it gets absolutely dark," and Tatan was ready—no, not so Gamelle. I wasted all my eloquence; but luckily a half-bottle of whisky inspired him with the courage my peroration had been unable to give him. We put the canoe into the water and after having been fiercely tossed, we arrived at the confounded cape. There more objections on the part of my friend Gamelle, whom I talked to this time with enough energy to keep him from having any answer to make. We doubled the Pointe au Sable,

* Here there is a French pun on the word "gamelle," which means mess.

and as soon as we were on the other side, the business became really serious: the waves were so powerful that in less than 5 minutes our vessel was completely full and we had just time enough to jump into the water and haul our canoe to the shore. There we spent a very unhappy night, soaked like ducks, and able to make scarcely any fire because of the rain coming down in torrents. In such a situation, I give my word, the lack of fire is a great misfortune, for one inevitable result of it is going hungry.

Next day it was fine weather till evening. We finished crossing the lake, and we made a good distance, because after leaving the lake the current grows strong. On the lake I saw the rock they call the Rocher à la Femme,* a rock made historic by a pretty Indian girl who threw herself from it. She was in love with a white man and her parents married her, or sold her, to a savage. But at the instant she was about to fall into the power of her master, she ran to the rock and began to chant the death-song. Her bridegroom seeing the tragedy threatening, rushed to prevent it, but she did not give him time, and throwing herself over the precipice, she was dashed to bits on the boulders bordering the lake. Where the devil will not sentiment build its nest!

* Maiden Rock.

The evening of the same day I had a storm so horrible, with so long and strong a tail to it, that the rain prevented my getting on. During three successive days I had rain and sun at intervals; but by night only incessant rain and nothing all night long but rain. I think this is much more disagreeable in a canoe than it is when you travel on foot or on horseback, because you are drenched both above and below. The only two things that disturb me, and I will not say that even those discourage me, when I travel, are vermin and rain. Vermin and insects that do not leave you a moment of peace by day or particularly by night, whose stings you not only have to try to defend yourself from, but also to complain of and scratch afterwards:—when you get up in the morning without having slept, and with your face, hands, almost your entire person swollen as if somebody had dipped you into boiling water; and the folds of your clothes, your leggings, all of you, full of the most disgusting sort of natural-history museum, especially if you have been unlucky enough to spend the night in an Indian wigwam—there is what I call demoralizing insects. And when I speak of bad weather, I do not refer to a storm that soaks you to the bones and then an hour or so later you get back home where you have other clothes and a good fire; but I mean a rain of 7 or 8 days never stopping, and during which your clothes and overcoat are wet through—when you go to bed in the mud in rain, with clothing still so drenched that it is useless to try to dry it at a fire, and everything gets a sour smell of must, and when you are in bed inside your soaking garments, a friendly little North wind blows till it freezes them into a nice sweet crust on top of you. Well, I had the bugs to amuse me during my whole land trip to the River St. Pierre, and the bad weather to keep up the fun during my whole voyage as far as Green Bay. That was almost all by canoe; and it was not until after the 14 October, or about that date, that it began to be cold but fine weather, which permits me to admire the beauties of Lake Michigan. It is on board the steamboat "Pennsylvania" that I am writing up my journal from little notes made in my pocketbook en route.

But let us return to my canoe and the Mississippi. The sun, appearing for a few instants, let me admire more perfectly the beauty of the upper Mississippi—its rocks, its hills, its lovely virgin forests where I have spent such miserable nights. The first few, or at any rate the first night one passes in the woods, one is quite amazed at the number and variety of noises one hears; and if not so fatigued, one would rather like to discover the cause of them all, or to fire a couple of shots at the wolves or the other denizens of the forest. But one soon gets used to all that.

On referring to the beauties of the Mississippi, I recall that after a great deal of rain I had one perfectly magnificent sunset. The sky was very brightly colored, the air clear and still. I was at that moment in my canoe not in the main stream of the Mississippi, but in one of the channels that are separated from the big one by charming islets. The current was fairly powerful, but made no sound. The woods were not too thick and allowed me to see the beauty and the gigantic proportions of the trees. The colors all about were very strong and the shadows most pronounced, so that with the imagination even lightly stirred, one could see there whatever one desired. And that day my imagination was violently stirred and all the sentimental part of my being was in a devilish turmoil. After having, it would seem, dreamed in silence, my heart was so full that I cried out: "What a beautiful sky! What a beautiful land! What a beautiful river!" Gamelle, the brave Gamelle, aroused by my exclamation, added: "Oh yes, sir; and what loads of ducks!"

On my honor, I believe that the chill of a dagger piercing my heart would have frozen me less and upset me less than his exclaiming; "What loads of ducks!" Translating it "what a big supper!" all sweet musings, all poetry was for me ruined.

Before getting to Lake Pepin I visited the Indian villages of Aigle Rouge and Tour des Pins and even the mouth of the River des Sauteurs.* After the lake I saw the remains of the village of La Feuille† whose unfortunate inhabitants were dead of smallpox. I passed near the mountain Trempe à l'Eau,‡ so named because, being a little peninsula, it dips into the water of the River des Serpents,§ a river well named, for the region it drains is infested by rattlesnakes. Those are in-

* The Sauters, or rather Saulters, were Chippewas from Sault Ste. Marie. The river separates Pepin and Buffalo Counties, Wisconsin, and is now called the Chippewa.

† La Feuille, the Leaf, was the famous Sioux chief Wabasha. Major Thomas Forsyth, in his Narrative of the Leavenworth Expedition (1819) in "Minn. Hist. Soc. Coll." III, 151, says ". . . we encamped six miles below *La Montagne qui trempe à l'Eau*. . . . We made the LEAF's village . . . a distance of only twelve miles." It must have been in Wabasha County, Minnesota. Edward Duffield Neill in his "History of Minnesota," Minneapolis, 1882, speaks of (p. xlviii) Winona "so lately the residence of Wapashaw" (*sic*).

‡ Now in Trempealeau County, Wisconsin.

§ Now the Trempealeau. If it was then called the Snake, the name probably referred to the Sioux and not to rattlesnakes.

deed rather common on the shores of the Mississippi. While crossing the prairies I saw several of the large snakes or adders that they call prairie-snakes. They are of a pretty large size, but not poisonous. Sometimes I shot at them, which made them leap in the strangest manner.

Near the River Méchante Hâche* some Indians called to us, and the two Canadians who knew a little Sioux, told me that they were inviting us to a banquet. I at once accepted their kind invitation, and a banquet of ducks and musk-rats was served to us. Curiosity led me to give the preference to the rats, and I was glad I had; for in the Fall the rat has lost almost all its flavor and tastes only just enough of musk to give an agreeable and aromatic suggestion of taste to the meat, which otherwise is much like that of rabbit.

My two companions showed me a rock that is greatly venerated among the Sioux and which they have painted with vermilion exactly as they do their own eyes, faces, and hair on feast-days or show occasions. I saw that Painted Rock,† so called because it had naturally some spots.

* Bad Axe River in Vernon County, Wisconsin.

† Painted Rocks, in Allamakee County, Iowa. However, "Red Rock, six miles below Saint Paul, receives its name from a boulder of granite which lies upon the shore of the Mississippi, and which the Indians have painted red and consider a tutelar

The etymology of the names of rivers, prairies, rocks, and other places in this country, derives, as one may have noticed, very often from some circumstance or souvenir connected with them, which passes from mouth to mouth and from generation to generation, and thus acquires a geographical authority. The funniest derivation I have heard of is that of the name of a prairie which the hunters along the Mississippi call the Ferribault (*sic*) Woman's Prairie. Here in a few words is the etymology:—Mr. Ferribault's wife was a half-breed who affected the costume and the customs of white people and made fun of Indians. Some young Indians in the neighborhood, vexed at her jokes, swore to be revenged, and one fine day they got hold of Mrs. Ferribault and, as the Indians say, passed her around on the prairie; and the chronicle has it that 25 young Indians inflicted upon her the most terrible punishment (from the moral point of view) that can be inflicted on a woman. Fortunately Mrs. Ferribault put up with all these outrages for the love of God and felt only the better afterwards.

When Heaven saw fit, I finally arrived at Prairie du Chien. A terrible, atrocious catas-

deity" ("Minnesota Year Book for 1851," St. Paul, p. 31), and Arese may have remembered that too.

trophe there awaited me. My fortitude and courage were almost shaken by it. My trunk had been robbed! Before leaving for the Indian country I had put all the best things I had into it: my dressing-case, the crown jewels and treasures, a letter of credit and recommendation, and all my papers. Everything had been taken! After two minutes of stupefaction and petrification, I burst not into tears but, I fear, into oaths and imprecations against Yankees; and that helped me a lot. Through precaution I had also put 1000 francs into that trunk, in case what I had on me might be stolen by the Indians. I made a firm resolve never in the future to be careful, for if I had kept all my belongings in my own care, the truth is that I should not have lost anything. As for what I still had, that was unfortunately very little—3 shirts and 3 scarves, no more stockings for a long while back. It was no longer a time to think of pebbles, minerals, Indian curiosities: they are not very useful against either cold or hunger. And still this event did not dishearten me enough to bring me to giving up the rest of my trip. I had only a few piastres left, but I did not care. I had been deserted even by my little hunting-shirt, which while I travelled had left me most underhandedly, bit by bit. So I bought myself a winter overcoat made of a woolen blanket, as the custom is in that part of the world; and I reckoned that by selling my fire-arms in Detroit, where I should need them no longer, I should have enough money to finish my trip.

I knew that letting them go would be as hard for me as giving the purest part of my blood; because really when you have good arms and they were given you by your intimate friends, weapons that have never failed to answer to your demands but have always faithfully served you, and have even perhaps got you out of some pretty serious scrapes, why, it is very difficult to give them up. It was then that I had to put my courage and firmness to the proof.

[IX]

Across Wisconsin Mostly in Canoes.

PRAIRIE DU CHIEN is a town in process of birth and one suspects that it has a hard time getting born, because for a long while it has not done so except on paper. I left the prairies and crossed the Wisconsin, to go see Mineral Point.* This name is appropriate for the whole district is very rich in copper and especially in lead mines. The part so far worked lies between the Wisconsin and the River des Fièvres,† the Mississippi, and the Illinois, an extent more than 100 miles square.

The excavations near Mineral Point are many but small—you would say like rat-holes—and that is because the government has sold the land in very small lots and each proprietor develops his own piece. Nevertheless the mines are very productive, for the ore in them is abundant and rich. It yields from 75 to 80 percent of pure metal, and in some places as much as 90 percent. I have been

* In Iowa County, Wisconsin.

† Now the Galena.

told that nearer to Galena and Dubuque the excavations are a great deal bigger.

From Mineral Point I went to Fort Winnebago. The country I went through to get there is most beautiful. Next to Virginia, it is the prettiest country I have seen in America. There are lovely prairies, very broken up and with high hills, sometimes crowned by rocks and firs: and the prairies are interspersed with fine forests, and from the hill-tops there are views as varied as they are extensive.

Fort Winnebago is like all the other American forts in the Indian country. It is between the Wisconsin and the Fox River, and is also called Portage, because it is necessary to carry all merchandise and canoes or other boats across by land, so that when they have come up by one river they can go down by the other as far as Green Bay, where they can then pass into the Great Lakes.

I happened to be there during the days when the American government commissioners were paying the compensation to the Indians for the purchase of their lands. There was a gathering of almost 4000 Indians, some Winnebagos, some Menominees. The American government buys land from the Indians by force if necessary, and pays them a few cents for it, surveys it, and resells it at 10 shillings. But that is not the only immoral thing about it: for instance this year the government pays them only half in money, and for the other half it sends them merchandise which apparently is such a drug that the Indians do not want it. To the government's injustice we must add the extortion and thieving of clerks and interpreters, who all try to outdo one another in that way. After that comes the demands of the whites for indemnities for damages sometimes imaginary and always exaggerated. Finally there are the shopkeepers that always flock to a place where payments are being made, and sell their goods at exorbitant prices. A fine idea those wretches must form of our civilization! Here is an instance of the gouging that goes on: I needed a mode of transportation for covering 50 miles; they asked me (they were white men) 65 piastres,* which is to say 344 francs, for hiring me a horse for only two days—and I no Indian, or at least so I flatter myself.

The Winnebagos—also called Puants,† because I suppose they are dirtier than other Indians—are the very scum of their race. They are more

* Probably he means dollars. Piastre was a name applied to various coins in various countries at various times.

† That is, in English, Stinkers.

treacherous, more malicious, more vindictive than the others. Their costume varies very little from the rest. Only, their women instead of having their hair down on the shoulders, like the Sioux women, wear it in a thick pigtail bound with colored ribbons and stuck with beads and other gewgaws. The men wear theirs rolled tight around the head and fastened with strings of Venetian glass trinkets, usually white, so that at a certain distance you would think they had eggs hung to their hair. The men wear wide embroidered garters below the knee, to hold their *mitasses* or loose leggings.

After a long search I found a miserable nag and a small cart, and left for the Butte des Morts.* But I had gone scarcely 12 miles before discovering that I should have difficulty in getting to my journey's end with that horse. Six miles farther I came to the Grande Rivière.† The water was high and the current pretty strong; indeed it was running rather too strong. I unloaded the little cart, with the help of the man who drove it I carried my scanty baggage to the other bank. Then the man stood up in the cart and urged his horse into the water. As far as halfway he went all right, and

* About where Oshkosh now is.

† This would seem to be the Fox.

then the poor beast was carried off by the current. The driver yelled "Help!" I jumped into the water, forgetting that I could not swim and moved solely by my guide's cries of distress. Before I had time to reach the horse, the current began to make me too move where it chose and not where I chose, and I saw myself lost. Fortunately I did not lose my nerve. I considered my position and realized that fighting against the current was useless; and at that instant I noticed that about thirty feet downstream the current hit the bank. I let myself go, and was lucky enough to get hold of the branches of a willow. So I was saved; and certainly had I not luckily noticed the situation, I should have been done for and have gone to help fatten the fishes in the Grande Rivière.

While this was taking place, which was a few seconds, the horse had got on the shore; but it had not the strength to drag the cart up, as the bank was high; and that task was for us. So while the driver held the cart, I got into the water and with a hatchet I hollowed out a sort of runway. Then we shoved our gala-coach and got it on dry land. But the horse came out of all this with one knee badly hurt, and I was forced, much against my will, to retrace my road as far as the Fort.

The country here is much like what I crossed

in first going to the Fort: always an enormous number of pheasants. Very often I saw them by as many as thirty together. Fortunately they were not timid, so that I always ate excellently.

At the Fort I found difficulties enough to give liver-complaint to a man with a liver of bronze; and a day lost would have made me miss the steamboat that I knew was due to be at Green Bay on such a date, and would have delayed my whole trip by maybe two or three weeks. The delay was nothing to me, for in those days unluckily for me, whether I lived well or badly in one place or another, was utterly indifferent to me; but my thirst for letters and for news from Europe was becoming more unbearable every moment. Some articles I had read in old American newspapers that I had fished out at various forts where I had passed, had got me devilish stirred up; without reckoning that for five months now I had had no news of my family. At last, after many disappointments, I found a family of Menominee Indians who were going down by canoe. I urged them very hard to take me along, and by means of 4 woolen blankets, 2 pounds of powder, and 4 pounds of shot, which I had bought at the Fort for 35 dollars, I got them to carry me to the Butte des Morts.

It was a very nice birch-bark canoe, 24 feet long by 3 or 4 wide at its greatest width. Such canoes are made of three pieces of birch-bark sewn together lengthwise and tarred along the seams. Inside there are little hoops of very thin wood to hold the bark tight, and the whole contrivance is so thin and so light that, other things being equal, it weighs no more than if it were made of pasteboard. I find that type of canoe far preferable to the wooden ones, because they are more comfortable to sit in, it is easier to move about, they are less tippy, and being infinitely lighter than the others, they always float on top of the waves and consequently never ship water. And for another even greater superiority—they go faster than the others. Their one bad point is that the least blow tears them, and to avoid that, you have to disembark when the water is extremely shallow, to keep them from rubbing along the bottom; and at times you have to lift them out and put them in again, so as not to risk destroying them against some bank of particularly dangerous character.

The family I travelled with consisted of an Indian man, his wife, and a boy of nine who also paddled. They were excellent savages, as all the Menominees are. The Menominees are also called the Wild Rice, from a sort of grain between oats and rice, which grows in their marshes and which they use a great deal of. I never travelled in the Indian country so comfortably as with that family. In Europe, according to what I have heard, travelling comfortably means having a good vehicle, a valet, a courier who pays the postilions pretty high to keep going, who sees about your lodgings, your dinner, your fire, your bed: but in my case it meant having a good canoe, a good matting, a tent, some good tinder and dry wood in order to be able to make a fire at once in spite of rain, having kettles and a whole well-run store. As for me, I had none of all that, but my Indians were well provided, and no sooner were we on shore than they had a tent put up with poles they cut and mats they carried in the canoe. Other mats were spread on the ground around a fire that was instantly lighted in the centre of the tent. The kettle, the kindly kettle, was instantly hung up, and ducks, game, or fish were put into it.

The best place in the tent and the nicest mat were always reserved for me. The two Indians were so unceremonious that my presence did not trouble them in the least, not even when they gave each other very positive proof of their conjugal affection, while I was smoking my pipe.

I crossed the Lakes du Boeuf and Lake Opacua,* and in three days I reached the Butte des Morts 125 miles away from Fort Winnebago.

One curious thing I noticed was that whenever the Indian or I had killed a duck or other bird and the Indian woman heard us or saw us loading our guns, she never failed to leave her paddle and to pluck a few feathers from the fresh-killed fowl and then to sprinkle them on the water. It was like a spell she was casting to bring luck to the shot we had prepared to fire next.

At the Butte des Morts (so called because of a massacre of Indians that took place at the time the French were occupying that region), there is now a post of the American Fur Company. The employee at the head of it told me that two days previous there had been a tragedy in his house. An Indian girl who was there had a quarrel with an Indian man. She seized a gun and shot him dead, and then ran to take refuge in her parents' wigwam; but they brought her back to be delivered to the dead man's family. When one member of a family is murdered, all the others have the right to avenge his death, and if they cannot find the culprit, the right is transferable, so to speak,

* The first named have become the Buffalo Lakes, and the other one, whatever it may then have been called, is now Lake Puckaway. They are in Marquette and Green Counties, Wisconsin.

against the whole family, unless, with the consent of the other family, they choose to buy off the price of blood with gifts. In that case the affair takes precisely the course of a civil contract. In the present instance the young girl's parents being too poor to pay and too feeble to fight, delivered their daughter up for death. But luckily the employee at the American Fur Company paid the blood-price and the girl was saved.

Here the Indian family left me. They were going in a different direction, and I found another canoe with two Indians, who in two days took me to Green Bay. I admit that at times, when I saw myself in that little canoe, quite alone with Indians in the very centre of North America, it struck me as funny; and on my word of honor I frequently thought I was dreaming. Indeed my social position really was singular and exceptional.

I crossed the Lake of the Butte des Morts, and the big Lake Winnebago, which is 13 leagues long and 4 wide. As the wind was favorable, we hoisted a blanket for a sail and made good progress. The second day we ran the rapids. The first two are rather long, several miles. They are not difficult. The swiftness with which you go through them is really astonishing. Sometimes far ahead you see water so shallow that as it dashes up it hardly covers the rocks, and you ask yourself: "Where the devil can this poor little canoe pass?" and in the time it takes to form the idea, the bad spot has gone by and you turn to look back at it, but in vain, for it is by then out of sight.

The noise of the third rapid, the most difficult one of all, could be heard from a long way off. It is more of a cataract than a rapid. According to what they told me, it is a league in length. You approach it with arrowlike speed. At the length of two musket-shots from the rapid I saw the Indian who was in the bow of the canoe rest his paddle on the boat. For an instant I supposed that having seen our vessel in a bad position among the rocks, he was going to leap out and try to swim ashore, leaving me there to fare as best I might. I seized my gun, for if through his behavior I was to leave unexpectedly for the other world, I wanted at least to send him on ahead of me so as to get decent lodgings ready for me. Suddenly I saw him take two little stones from the powder-sack he wore around his neck. One of them he tossed to the right and the other to the left of the canoe, took up his paddle again, and we shot the rapids splendidly. He was casting a charm, just as at home, priests in the country give a benediction from the church door to charm away storms and chase off hail. Once you feel sure there is no danger, it is great fun to feel the little canoe leaping along the waves like a carp and flying as fast as thought! Sometimes she shipped a bit of water by the bow. The water coming down with great speed, is broken on those rocks that are just on the surface, and forms waves that travel in the opposite direction to the current; and those meeting the canoe that arrives with the swiftness of lightning, give it a terrific shake and sometimes fill it.

At the fourth rapid we made a portage of a quarter of a mile. That is, we were obliged to carry the canoe on our backs. After that I descended the river to its outlet, and that evening I arrived at Green Bay. The next morning at ten o'clock I left for Chicago. I had time to visit the growing town, which did not require many minutes. I excused myself from going to see the Fort, for all the forts are alike. They are nothing but small barracks, built sometimes of stone, but oftener of wood. One of my acquaintances who had gone to see the Fort some days before, told me that the garrison was 9 men strong (including the drummer and the officer), five of whom were that day under arrest.

[X]

Apologia for Taking the Trip & a Description of the Indians.

I LEFT on the "Steam Packet Pennsylvania," which is not a good ship. On the contrary, she is dirty and poorly run: you would think yourself on some European steamboat, between London and Calais, or Dover and Ostend, rather than on an American one, because generally those are lovely. There were 640 passengers on board, a regular little Tower of Babel, except for a dozen well-bred people, among whom I do myself the honor of counting myself, although my ruined clothes would not give me the right to—and about a dozen more who permitted themselves the sweet illusion that they were well-bred too, but who really were not. The rest were nothing but a horrible mixture of Irish, Germans, and Kentuckians or something resembling them. To top the bad luck there were masses of small children howling, not to tear your heart, but your ears. And nursing mothers! An odor and a scene to disgust a stomach made of Corinth metal which is the hardest metal known. I more than once cried: "Oh, how much better off I was when sleeping on the prairies, or in the forest, and even under a heavy rain!" Despite all that, I must admit that I had a feeling of joy on finding myself aboard a steamboat, after all the trouble and all the discomforts I had borne and all the vexations and obstacles I had met. I seemed to be home once more. The pleasurable emotion I felt later, on stepping foot on board one of the magnificent American *packets* which carried me back toward my native land, was not a great deal stronger.

But what the devil, you will say to me, did you go way off there for, to the end of the world, to run so many dangers, suffer so much fatigue and privation; and what good did it do you, you who are neither geologist, mineralogist, nor naturalist? As I see it, the reply is fairly simple: I believe it is not absolutely necessary to be something ending in "ist," in order to be capable of seeing, feeling, and admiring the beauties of nature. Besides, I trust that every one is free to take his pleasure where he finds it. There are people who find it in being "fashionable" in London or "incroyable" in Paris. But I, on the contrary, find it in roving about either with a caravan of Arabs in the deserts of Africa or with Indians on the Western Prairies.

A life of adventure guided almost by pure chance, has a charm that no one can conceive who has not tried it. It is quite true that by evening of the first days I passed on the prairies my senses were all excessively fatigued because of the continual tension they were subjected to. For it was necessary to listen for the slightest sound, and as soon as eyes freed from any obstacle could take in the full sweep of an immense prairie, it was necessary to look very close so as to be sure whether there was smoke to be seen, or footprints, whether the grass was just alike everywhere and motionless, whether I don't know what. But by the end of three or four days I was as well habituated to all that as to the idea that my existence depended on the sight of my musket or that of my pistols. In the course of my life I have always had the good luck or bad luck to accustom myself very rapidly to all circumstances. I say good or bad luck, because when the circumstances were disagreeable, their unpleasantness did not last long, and when they were agreeable, their charm and in particular their novelty did not last long either. Probably people will do me the honor to believe that it requires a lot of courage to make such a trip. That is not so in the least: but it does require lots of persistence.

The time courage was necessary was in New York where, having a pleasant place to live, being well received in Society and much entertained, having friends and all kinds of attractions in life, I spread out on my bed, for the table was not big enough, a huge map of America and said to myself: "I will give up all the comforts of my present existence and go live amidst privations and dangers." That is the moment when perhaps I did have to use courage. But afterwards the rest was nothing but a consequence, and in this lower world, when one wishes a thing one must also wish its consequences. Otherwise one can never wish anything.

At Saint Louis they tried to weaken my decision: the managers of the American Fur Company gave me a very unattractive picture of what awaited me and admitted what they feared for me, which was that I should probably remain forever somewhere on the road. I don't know if it is fortunate or not, but I have always had a very firm or a very stubborn character (one may choose the adjective one likes: it makes no difference to me; I am not fussy about words). The fact is that I did not like to relinquish my decision: so, having made all the purchases requisite for such a trip and put aside in my trunk the famous 1000 francs (which, one will remember, the devil stole), I considered it my strict duty to spend 300 fr., or about that, during the last two days, so as not to have any regrets in case of fatal accidents; and I departed with a light heart and an empty purse.

Travelling on the prairies can never be made very comfortable; but for money one may have tents, extra horses, huntsmen to bring in game and to form an escort. But since unfortunately for me my communications with my minister of finance were not direct, I had to do without all that, and my cloak, my legs, and my musket bore all the work.

One of the great advantages I gained from my trip was a tremendous confidence in myself—the conviction that nothing in the world could make me shrink, and that in whatever case, I should always be able to be sufficient to myself, especially from the point of view of morale.

Before diving back into the civilized world, and after having seen Indians en masse and of all varieties, after having travelled and lived with them, and particularly after having become sick and tired of them, I will try to write a couple of words about them.

Without venturing into a scientific question

which is perhaps superfluous and certainly far beyond my powers and my knowledge, I will yet say that the scholars who have examined the monuments and the hieroglyphic inscriptions found in Mexico and in the interior of the United States, decided that the natives who were found in those places at the period of the discovery of the New World, were not the first inhabitants, without however being able to discover anything about their origin. As to the Indians of today, it seems to be generally agreed that they descend from Tartar Mongols who, in very distant times, came over from Kamchatka across the Aleutian and the Kurile Islands and Behring Straits, to the American continent. Of several Indian tribes very powerful not more than a century since, there now remain only the names; and such is the lot reserved also for the tribes that still drag their wretchedness through the deserts and prairies of America.

The white men who were so well received at the time of the discovery of the American continent, are the cause of their destruction. Firearms, iron, liquor, corruption, and disease, all introduced as means of so-called civilization, are the loss of those unhappy tribes. To that one must add that the Indians, not knowing agriculture, are obliged to feed themselves entirely by hunting, and that, being pushed back by the whites toward the Rocky Mountains, they find game there, it is true, but at the same time also find other tribes who dispute their right to hunt it; so that the only choice left them is between hunger, violence, the white men, and war—war to the death in case they go forward.

Today the number of Indians in North America—and by that I mean not only the United States, but the whole North American continent—has been reduced to less than a million. The number of Indians in the territories of the United States, from its frontiers to the Rocky Mountains, is about 500,000. This reckoning is maybe not very exact, for among the thousand difficulties of making a count there is the very great one of the continual fluidity of those brave men who are always moving, whether because they are driven, or because, in order to hunt, they are obliged to follow after their game which flees in fright before the white man's axe. These Indians are divided into several tribes, each one of which has its own slight variations of appearance, religion, language, mores, and politics; but the differences are not very marked. I went through various tribes, but the one whose ways and habits I know best, is the Sioux tribe, for it is among them that I stayed longest.

As to their religion, the Indians believe in the existence of a superior, a supreme Being whom they call "the Great Spirit" or "Manitou," whose name they swear by, and to whom they address prayers, but very rarely and only in important crises. They believe also in the immortality of the soul, but they have no idea of its spirituality; the good creatures are too material to conceive of that. They believe also in eternal rewards and punishments: that is to say, if a brave warrior has killed a great many enemies, if he has been courageous and a good hunter, when he comes to die they believe he has departed for a far country beyond the mountains or the great lake (which in their language is as much as to say the Ocean), and that there he will find beautiful women, abundance of game, good horses, good pasturage and springs of clear water. The relatives or the friends of the deceased kill his best horse and a few enemies or slaves to serve him in his new abode. Whereas the coward on the contrary, leaves for a barren region, without game and lacking everything that, in their eyes, makes up the charm of existence.

There are however some tribes among which

the missionaries have penetrated and sown the principles of the Gospel; which after the missionaries' departure have unfortunately, by the lapse of time and the influence of tradition from father to son, been so disfigured and mixed with former practices and customs, that they now present a religion and a morality nothing more than absurd and grotesque; so that it requires the keen and trained eye of an observer to dig something of the Gospel out of them. The only favorable result has been that the habits of those tribes are less cruel, less sanguinary. Sometimes the Indians adore a stone, a rock, a tree, but in general fetichism is not widespread.

Usually the savages have great respect for the dead, whom they expose for some while on wooden scaffoldings, and whom they then bury along with their arms in tombs, little artificial mounds of earth; and for several days afterwards they bring them something to eat. They attach a religious idea to dreams too, without however knowing how to explain them. Generally they accept them as a sign of something about to happen. They have faith in witchcraft and attach great importance to casting spells in order to make this event happen and that one not happen.

Their form of government is an aristocratic

republic, with a chief whose eminence is sometimes hereditary, sometimes elective. Elections among them and changes of chiefs, take place very tranquilly and little by little.

It very frequently happens that in some tribe a bold young warrior, enterprising and lucky, brings off a number of expeditions, killing many enemies without losing too many of his own warriors (for that they hold by enormously), and begins gradually to acquire influence and to become chief in fact if not in name, and by degrees the former chief is forsaken and the new one recognized in his stead.

The tribal affairs and treaties of peace and war are discussed and decided by a majority vote in a general Council, where they smoke and talk a great deal; in these Councils there are always renowned orators who, I have been assured, are very logical and very decisive.

All private differences are settled by an agreement arranged by arbiters who usually are chosen from among the two parties' friends. The punishment of crimes is left to the individuals concerned without any form of trial. Crimes against members of one's own tribe (against those of another tribe crimes count as bravery and skill) limit themselves to theft, murder, cowardice, and sorcery. A person robbed has the right to recover, if he can, not only his property but everything besides that he is able to take from the one who robbed him. A murderer is put to death by the victim's family; but sometimes there are settlements, that is to say, presents, which are, so to speak, blood-money; and sometimes the transfer of a prisoner of war, who if he is adopted by the family, takes the dead man's place and position. If a homicide has been committed during a state of drunkenness, or by accident, the guilty person is not responsible; but for some time he voluntarily keeps himself hidden or apart, condemns himself to fasting, and does not approach his wife. An Indian who has been guilty of cowardice is punished with death by his own family (what a good example even for a civilized nation!). Those suspected of witchcraft can expect no safety but by running away from the tribe, for if they are caught, they will be mercilessly put to death and with their families' consent, who would be very careful to make no opposition lest they should thus render themselves accessaries in the crime and sharers in the penalty.

Hunting, as the sole means of subsistence, and war, as the dominant passion and instinct, are the only two ideas well developed among the savages. Consequently everything that could be called science or art, can, with some slight exceptions, be said not to exist for the Indian. I was amazed to observe that they understood nothing about the movements of the stars. The colors of stones, the appearance of trees and bark, as indicating the South and the North, are the only guidance they have when they travel.

Medicine is professed among them by magicians; but every Indian knows how to use several very efficacious simples; guaiacum for snake-bites, sassafras, certain bitter herbs for fever, steam-baths, which I have spoken of above, for rheumatism, and blood-letting for inflammations are all known to them. The instrument for letting blood is made of a piece of wood into which they set an animal's tooth, or a fish-bone, or a pebble, which they wrap with skin or string so as to leave only as much sticking out as is requisite for piercing the vein without injuring the arm.

The Indians are very capable at dressing wounds by applications of herb poultices active enough to draw out pieces of bone and even leaden bullets, no matter how deep-lodged they may lie; I have seen men who had been pierced straight through by gun-shot or by arrows and had been cured: and that without the least knowledge of anatomy or any other science.

The training of children among the savages lasts a very short while. As soon as they are able to look after their own needs, or at least to stand on their legs, they have entire freedom and live with their parents as with strangers, receiving from the father nothing except lessons in courage, slyness, and revenge—practical lessons, of course, not merely theoretic.

The Indians may marry as many wives as they are able to feed. Usually they buy them from their parents. The wife has an entirely passive role, she is almost the slave of her husband. It is she who cooks the meals, takes care of the babies, the tents, the horses, and in a word, the whole establishment. When her husband is away at war or hunting, it is she who tans the skins and the furs and tailors the clothes. On the trail it is the wife that carries the babies, and the baggage, and attends to all the work connected with camping. The husbands are jealous or pretend to be jealous and cut off the noses and the ears, sometimes even kill wives that have failed to be faithful. The wives' behavior is in general pretty regular, whereas that of girls is not in the least so. A girl gives or sells herself to anybody she chooses, and does it almost *coram populo*, without her reputation's suffering the slightest bit. When a stranger arrives in a tribe and is well received, it never fails that he is given a woman for the time he is to be there. In any case, supposing he wants one, he need not lack. "Running the match" is a phrase in use among the Canadian hunters: it is one of the better methods for getting girls, and the pursuit goes like this:

You enter a tent when the fire there is out. You have been careful to have a torch in your hand, or it would be better to say, a lighted piece of wood. You go along past the different girls in bed, and the one who puts it out, receives you in her arms. That is how it is sometimes done; but ordinarily you just go into a tent where you know there is a pretty girl, you stir up the fire so as to be able to pick her out among the other people, you bring her a present of a mirror, some glassware, a knife, or any other little thing, and your happiness is assured.

In general the savages do not know the charm of mystery and consider the actual formula with which one gives proof of lively emotion as an animal function and nothing more.

As I have said above, when I was travelling with an Indian family, the husband would prove to his wife, before me, the lively interest she aroused in him; and that in a little tent twelve feet square, while I was tranquilly smoking my pipe, and no more embarrassed than if it had been the cat.

The language spoken by the savages varies with the tribes. Great scientific questions have been raised in regard to its origin. About the parent tongue and about the points of resemblance in the languages I have read a great deal without understanding anything. The only thing positive is that the languages are always nasal, guttural, and aspirated; in short, they are very disagreeable to the ear, above all to mine which are content to detest aspirated languages.

The Indians are in general fine-looking and well-made although a bit slender, and one sees that the prime element in their construction is agility rather than strength. Their skin is the color of wrought copper or of mahogany. In the South it is a bright red and toward the North it has an olive tinge. Their faces are regular and sometimes would be almost beautiful and noble, if they did not go to so much pains to ruin them by trying to beautify them. They tattoo some parts of their bodies and frequently make lines on both cheeks. Their hair is black, thick, and stiff like horsehair. Their eyes are black and when they are excited, lively; but habitually sullen and impassive. It is difficult to give an exact idea of their costume, seeing that it varies extremely according to tribe and to personal caprice. The Sioux wear their hair long and falling to their shoulders, decorated with little beads, colored feathers, bits of carved horn or bone. In other tribes the head is shaved except for a little lock or braid hanging on the shoulder. Others shave their heads and retain only a sort of crest. Sometimes they dye their hair red, grey, and even occasionally with mud. Their ears are nearly always pierced in several places, and through the little holes they stick rings, ribbons, small beads, or other ornaments, whose weight makes the ear droop down on itself like a hunting-dog's. In some tribes it is a distinction to have holes in the ears and to have a little black spot on the forehead or on the chin. In each tribe there is only one person privileged to make embellishments, and those who have been decorated are superior to the others.

It is however a pitiable fatality that aristocracy has made its poison infiltrate even among the savages, and this is nothing but a moneyed aristocracy, for they pay dear for that right. The sole reasonable aristocracy, that of personal merit, is also recognized by the Indians. Their brave warriors wear ornaments at the neck, insignia indicating the number of men they have killed or horses stolen, either in beads or shells, or even rather often a small bit of mirror. One very strange thing—among the Indians it is the men who are the most coquettish, the vainest. A male Indian is capable of remaining for hours together in front of a piece of mirror, whereas the women almost never make use of one. The mirrors serve for telegraphs, and when the sun is shining they can send instantaneous signals that are visible at a vast distance, as for example from one end of a prairie to the other.

The Indians wear no beard. Some keep a sort of imperial, which falls from the chin; but in general they cut their beards with a knife, as close as possible, then with a piece of iron or brass wire wound very tight around a stick. When the stick is removed, the wire forms a sort of spring which serves to take off all the hairs down to the roots. The same instrument is used by both sexes (which can scarcely be very amusing).

The Indians wear bracelets which are just a wire roughly carved. The upper part of their bodies is bare, or sometimes in Winter they put on a sort of shirt made of deerskin and large stockings that come up to the top of their thighs, embroidered in colored leather, in porcupine quills, or for the great warriors in slain enemies' scalps. They fasten the big leggings above their hips with a strap, to which they attach a piece of cloth or leather (before and behind) passing between their legs and always kept on even when they are in their simplest negligee. That part of their costume is called a "brayet."* Hung to their belt they always carry their scalping-knife, their tomahawk, and their pipe. As footgear they have boots of buffalo hide or deer, which are tight around the lower part of the leg. These are embroidered and have no soles, and are called "moccasins." The Indians closest to the white men have an unattractive fashion of wearing blankets as a wrap, and the others have them of buffalo leather ornamented and embroidered and with their exploits indifferently painted on the inside: the number of men killed, white and red, specifying whether killed with arrow, gun, or tomahawk (which has great merit), and the men among the enemy whom they have touched, for it is a great feat of hardihood to dash madly away and plunge into the enemies' midst and return after having merely touched one of them, without even having done

* The real word is "brayette," a variant of "braguette."

him the least harm. Their weapons are the *tomahawk,* a sort of little hatchet, and the bow and arrows. Many have muskets, or lances made of a pole 6 feet long, to which is fixed a sort of big knife-blade 1½ feet long.

The women wear their hair smooth, parted on the forehead and falling over the shoulders. They wear a little skirt of blanket or leather, which they attach above the hips with a strap. Their corsage is formed by the same piece as the skirt and held up by a pair of small suspenders passing over the shoulders. Others wear a skirt separate from the waist, and in that case the skirt is held in the same way by a belt which is covered by the skirt falling back over it: as to the waist it is a sort of sleeveless waistcoat. The skirts come halfway to the knee. For stockings they wear a *mitasse* or embroidered leggings which come to the knee: for shoes, moccasins. On their backs they wear either a blanket or a skin, which covers them from head to foot. When they can have their clothes of blanket, red is the favorite color. On the trail they carry a baby, sometimes even two, inside the blanket on their back, and supported by the top of the head.

The women's costume is perhaps more picturesque than the men's.

[XI]

On the Great Lakes from Green Bay to Buffalo. Also Niagara Falls.

Now let us return to our steamboat, which from Green Bay took me to Chicago, and on board of which I had thc pleasure of meeting one of my New York acquaintances, Mr. Peter Schermerhorn, an amiable and well-educated young man, who let me share his stateroom.

Since everybody in America does something, Mr. Schermerhorn builds cities, and not merely on paper as is somewhat the style, but of real masonry and quite seriously, and he does a very good business. There was also on board a theatrical company on its way to Chicago, whose two conspicuous members were the leading lady and the head dancer. Mrs. or Miss Ingerson, for I am not certain which, was neither young nor good-looking, but indeed quite the contrary; but to make up for that she paced the deck with an air of as much importance as either Semiramis or Cleopatra could have worn. The dancer, who called herself French, or more truly advertised herself as French, had apparently had terrible misfortunes with her shoes, whether low or high, for she wore a pair of her husband's boots, and such was the slimness of her legs, which would have done credit to a fighting-cock, and the fulness of her dresses, that you might have called her a butterfly-in-boots.

Because of a heavy wind we were unable to leave Green Bay the first day, and spent the night anchored there.

Next morning we sailed out of Porte des Morts, which takes its name from an accident in which 40 canoes and everybody in them were lost; we saw Milwaukee and Racine, two infant towns, each nicely situated on the bank of a river; and afterwards we arrived at Chicago, a very pretty little town, which is almost at the lower end of Lake Michigan and on the banks of the Chicago River.

Although in reality the town has not yet 44 streets lengthwise and 42 crosswise, as it is made to have on the map, still it is an astonishing place. 4 or 5 years ago it was nothing but an Indian village, and now it is a very pretty little town of 6000 inhabitants, with good shops, fine streets having sidewalks, quays, a magnificent hotel, a theatre, four churches of different denominations, and a great many handsome houses built of stone. Considering the importance of the position, Chicago is destined to become a great city. They are already making a canal to give the lake communication with the Mississippi:* a work that would be gigantic in a peopled and organized country, and which becomes truly fabulous in a region like this which is still, so to say, in a savage condition.

When speaking of America one might certainly find something bad to say of her, and especially is it easy to sharpen one's wit by finding objects of ridicule here—that is a commodity not lacking: but if one has only just a tiny bit of candor, he must put his conceit into his pocket and European as he may be, say that this is an astounding country, magical, miraculous; and that ever so many things here must be seen to be believed; and that things nobody would dare to dream of in Europe, things that would be rejected as absurd, and *that* in spite of all our resources—well, in this country, no sooner conceived, no sooner carried out! and with means as small as the enterprising courage of the Americans is assuredly large—and by small means I refer principally to the scant population.

*This project is mentioned in the "Gazetteer of the State of Missouri." Alphonso Wetmore, 1837, p. 190.

During the voyage we passed close enough to land to see the fine country bordering the lake. It consists of thinly wooded prairies. A contrary wind and rough water kept the steamboat an extra day at Chicago, and a scene took place between the second-in-command and some of the passengers which proves the truth of what I was saying above about the droll, the too droll mob we had aboard. The Irish in a somewhat animated discussion with the mate, fell upon him *en masse*; but he who was pretty well built, with the aid of one of the ship's men, put 5 or 6 of the Irishmen out of the fight. Still, at the last, the two heroes were overcome by numbers. The officer was afterwards very sick in bed, and it would seem that his interior workings were most violently upset: the other man had a broken head. That night, for fear that the Irish, who had gone ashore, should return and attack the steamboat, arms and ammunition were distributed to the crew and to passengers, and men were left on guard. Everything was ready, except the Irish, who only came and walked about on the dock and then very quietly went home, in order, I imagine, to put blotting-paper soaked in vinegar-water on the bruises they had received in the morning. If the Irish had come aboard, there would have been fighting, there would have been many mishaps to deplore, and certainly the public authorities would according to their noble custom, have taken notice of nothing, either before, during, or after. Is it a good thing or a bad, this absence or at any rate blank silence, of any law, considering that law's duty is to protect, defend, and revenge society in case of attacks by individuals? Another question I asked myself, and which I will also answer further on when I have the time and when moreover I have the inclination to chat about economics and public rights, is whether America would not prosper more under a stronger government, under a government that would give a common direction to all the partial efforts that now branch out right and left and sometimes without rhyme or reason, and which from time to time produce partial or even general crises. Perhaps the progress would not be so swift, but surely it would be solider, more positive, and would give more guarantees for the future. For it must not be forgotten that the so much vaunted progress of the American Confederation depends on many contingent causes that will have ceased to exert any influence in a future nearer at hand than most people think.

Among these causes we must put in the first line the vastness of area, the newness of political institutions, the almost continuous renewal of the population whose ancient seed (if I may be allowed the expression) is receiving a constantly fresh fructification from European immigration.

When the area is diminished through settlements being scattered over it, when the institutions have aged and will therefore be struggling against the efforts at reform that are the forerunners of revolution, when the population more anciently established on the soil is forced to secure its rights and privileges against the immigrants in whom it will no longer be able to see assistants but merely competitors very troublesome and very much to be feared, then the American Confederation will find itself placed in nearly the same circumstances as our old European societies; then it will have to tighten the reins of government, at the risk of overthrowing the Holy Ark of its Constitution, for it is only the strong and solid governments that are able to live. History is there to prove it to us—as well as the kingdoms and the republics!

At Chicago we landed the theatrical troupe and almost all our passengers. Others came aboard, but in smaller numbers. The bad weather, which still lasted, gave me a chance to visit the town in detail.

I saw a foundry, a steam flour-mill, a steam saw-mill for making window-frames, public schools, several printing-presses, reading-rooms where the three daily papers are on file, a post-office, several stagecoach lines that serve a still almost savage region, and a number of steamboats, some topsail schooners,* and various other things; and all this in a town that has existed only five years! How many cities in Europe that count centuries and twenty to thirty thousand souls, are backwards in civilization in an ignominious manner, compared to this little town? Shame, shame and curses upon those governments which, moved solely by a sordid avarice and by the thirst for power, not only do not incite but even with all their strength retard the development and the natural progress of nations, and which in place of wise and liberal institutions, burden nations with castes, nobles, monks, a police that violates instead of protecting the citizens' rights, and which in a word, encourage what one may very correctly call the vermin of society!

At last the wind fell a bit and toward evening

* The text says "bricks seunners," obviously the second word is meant for schooners. According to the "Technical Dictionary of Sea Terms," etc., William Pirrie, London, 1921, a brick-schooner is the same thing as a brick-goëlette and that in English is a topsail schooner.

the third day we left Chicago. We were very comfortable on board with not over a hundred passengers, most of whom did not leave their berths although we were on a lake, which, parenthetically is nearly as large as the Mediterranean. We passed near the Manitou Islands, the Fox Islands and the Beaver Islands, all of which might better be called large sand-banks, very lofty and offering nothing to look at except sand-dunes and a very miserable vegetation—a few wretched, skinny shrubs and nothing else. The shore of Lake Michigan is like that everywhere. We arrived at Mackinaw Island, which is at the other end, 300 miles distant from Chicago. This island is situated between Lakes Michigan and Huron, and almost opposite the St. Mary's River, which forms the outlet for the water of Lake Superior. The island is very well placed and has an attractive appearance. Its summit is crowned by a fortification from which you get a very pretty view. The island's great curiosity is a natural arch hollowed in a rock. There are still Indians to be seen there, a remnant of the Ottawas, and they make very nice reed mats and different objects in bark. I left the island by night; but the boat was surprised by a storm and had to put in at Presque Isle, where I saw a very fine land-locked bay. The storm having lulled a little, we managed to make the length of Lake Huron. We entered the St. Clair River, crossed Lake St. Clair, and finally arrived at Detroit, a pretty and flourishing town, which I perhaps found prettier than it really is for the reason that, after three months' total deprivation of letters, I there found a huge package of them.

The next evening on board another steamboat I left Detroit. Although I had frequcntly changed my river, my boat, my lake, the weather never changed, and two hours after our departure it was once more very bad. I was in my cabin re-reading and digesting my letters at ease, when a terrific bump distracted me. I said, "Now we have run aground," and although I was astonished that that should happen in a lake, I went on reading. I also heard men shouting and moaning, but about that too I bothered myself very little. But when I heard someone shout that they were to take the axes forward, my curiosity was so much aroused that I admit I left my letters, to discover what was going on. They had neglected to light the signal at the bow, and as the night was very thick and very black, an unlucky schooner cut across our path, not noticing the presence of a steamboat until too late. The bow of our boat getting entangled in the schooner's rigging, broke off its bowsprit and one of the schooner's masts, and the broken beams and the tangled sails and ropes of both vessels, were the reason for the command to bring the axes. In a moment everything was in order again; but it was a little like the order that prevailed at Warsaw,* for the steamboat, slightly damaged, was hardly free before she started ahead again, and the unlucky schooner, unmasted and with men wounded on board and in very heavy weather, got out of the scrape as she could. I chose to believe, for my part, that she got out of it marvellously. As soon as the steamboat was under way again, I returned to my letters—I had 34 of them. They gave me both good and bad news, and I will spare my unfortunate reader my private emotions.

On Lake Erie we saw Cleveland, a pretty little town, which will before long be a very important one.

We also passed Grand River, Ashtabula, and Conneaut,† other towns, or to speak more pre-

*In 1831 after the Russians had battered the Poles into obedience, the French Foreign Minister, Marshal Sébastiani, informed the Deputies: "Gentlemen, order now reigns at Warsaw."

† Fairport and Richmond (afterwards New Market) were both at the mouth of the Grand River halfway between Cleveland

cisely, other localities where there is everything required for constituting a town, except two things: houses and people;—for there were streets to be seen all marked out and with name-posts, and all christened with high-sounding names, the beginning of a railway or a canal, a post-office, a church, a school, one or two wooden cottages. This reminded me of a story that happened to one of my friends. He was shooting snipe in the swamps in the North of New York State, and saw a half-dozen persons with papers in their hands, who were shouting. His curiosity was touched and he granted a short armistice to the snipe while he went to see what it was all about. They told him they were auctioning bids for building the Town Hall. "But what Town Hall?" he asked. I no longer remember what grandiose name he heard in answer to his question? Certainly some antique name. Rome or Athens at least. My friend inquired, "Where is the town?" "You are in it, sir;" and he was in mud up to his hips. Note that there are a great many towns of the same kind in the United States.

and Ashtabula. There does not appear to have been a town called Grand River. As for Conneaut, which in the text is "Concat," maybe its name was too much for others besides Arese. At any rate, it would seem to have been changed into Salem.

After having crossed Lake Erie I reached Buffalo, which is not a town of the kind I have been mentioning, but a handsome city, well-built and already rather extensive, and containing perhaps the best hotel in America; and I confess that after having fasted and eaten badly for 4 or 5 months, I found that a good dinner has, in its way, its charm and its poetry.

During my trip I had plenty of time to verify a sort of axiom, which says that civilization has a direct connection with the tines of a fork. Truly, the savages among whom there is a complete absence of civilization, eat with their fingers, consequently without forks; when civilization begins to make its influence felt, comes the knife, which we may well call a one-tined fork; then comes the big iron fork with two tines; then those with three; and last of all, when one has the happiness to encounter a four-tined silver fork, one may be sure of being in an eminently civilized country.

From Buffalo I went to Niagara Falls. Any description of them is impossible. I stayed there 5 days and I ended my stay only because everything in this world must have an end: otherwise I should probably be there still.

The more one looks at the astounding spectacle, the more astonished he becomes, the more it appeals to him, the more beauty he finds in it. I visited every part of it conscientiously and in detail, on this side and on that, above and below, in good and in bad weather, by sunshine and by moonlight, and it is always sublime and magnificent. Without possible contradiction, the finest views are the one from Table Rock and the one from a certain spot on the railway to Lewiston, from where you see the Falls at a distance among the trees, like a magnificent miniature framed. The one disappointment you have is when you go to see the Grotto of Aeolus [Cave of the Winds], which is under the little Falls. They tell you that it is worth seeing, that you can go a good way in—that is, 60 or 80 steps—under the big ones. You put on a special costume of oiled cloth, you go in clutching on to the rocks, in a rain and a wind that there is nothing to resemble; you are obliged to cover your mouth with one hand so as to breathe, and with the other you cling to the rocks so as not to pitch into the gulf; and after having taken the devil of a lot of trouble and risked killing yourself at every step, you come out again without having seen anything at all, because the water that inundates you prevents your distinguishing one object from another.

To give an idea of the Falls, I will add that they

are a mile and three quarters wide and from 160 to 172 feet high, and it is calculated that the thickness of the water at the moment of falling, is from 20 to 24 feet. It is the overflow from the four big lakes that leaps over there to get into Lake Ontario.

I went to look at a lot of things I shall not speak of because they are not worth the trouble. The one exception I shall make will be for the Whirlpool, which is a rapid at the foot of the Falls, where the water boils up so violently that its level in the middle of the river is 8 or 9 feet above that at the edges. I don't know whether there really is that difference or whether it is an optical illusion, but people in the town assured me that the calculation is correct and not at all exaggerated.

The guide who conducts visitors (that is to say, those of them that want a guide) to see the Falls, has a visitors' book. Among the curious things I read in it, I could not refrain from copying what Captain Marryatt* had written: "Upon a patient and careful examination of the Falls called Niagara, I have come to the conclusion that if any person were to be taken down in them, he would

*Very likely Marryatt had written it not long before, as he was in America that year, 1837. From the famous diary we learn that Philip Hone had had him to dinner on May 19.

be in considerable danger of receiving serious injury!"*

A thing that sometimes amused me and at other times irritated me extremely was to see the gross and stupid way in which some visitors observed this marvel of nature.

Chance alone brought such visitors to Niagara, because that was their shortest route. Accordingly they arrived on the run, saw the sights on the run, and left in the same way so as not to be late for dinner; and very often, finding me perched on a rock somewhere overlooking the Falls, where I passed my whole time, they would ask me what there was to see, and I would tell them the different spots worth going to. Too frequently they considered those too far away, and sometimes after having examined the cascade for a couple of minutes, they would ask me, with an utterly American calm and coolness: "Oh, is that Niagara?" Thank you for nothing!

* In English in the original.

[XII]

Canada. Then via Lake Champlain, the Hudson, & the Sound, to Boston.

WITH many regrets and much against my inclination I left Niagara. I departed on board an English steamer, to go see Upper Canada. "What a difference," a good American who happened to be on board too, said to me with a triumphant air, "between an American and an English steamboat!"—"Yes," I replied, "the difference is immense. Yours are finer, better built, speedier. But what a difference in everything else besides! Here you have a clean tablecloth, berths with nice white sheets, a napkin apiece, good table service, the plates changed for every course, silver forks; the captain and all the personnel on board pleasant and obliging to the passengers, all of them things that would seem mythological and fabulous on an American steamboat." The dear man was terrified, turned on his heel with a pirouette, and shot off without adding a syllable. That is because (damn it all!) there was nothing to answer.

I went to Toronto, the capital of Upper Canada, a town with a population of 12,000, built somewhat in the English style, as indeed are all the towns of Upper Canada, whereas those in Lower Canada are rather more in the French taste.

On leaving Lewiston I saw the monument to the memory of General Brooks; nothing remarkable. I visited Kingston where there are a Fort and an Arsenal from which in time of war come seventy-fours, frigates, and other smaller warships. I also saw other little towns and villages, which offered nothing interesting or unusual.

The St. Lawrence River from Kingston to Prescott is majestic. The banks are high, the rocks magnificent, cedars and spruces of the greatest beauty ornament the shores, the water is very clear and of a lovely dark green. The stretch called the Thousand Islands is most picturesque: there the river is so very wide that you can hardly ever see both banks, being prevented by the huge number of little islands, and the rocks there are of a charming effect. Although I admire the St. Lawrence very much, still I prefer the Mississippi, of course I mean the upper Mississippi. Its banks are loftier and more majestic, and in general its scale is more grandiose. Magnificent as these rivers may be, the banks of the Rhine lose nothing by comparison with them. I even find the Rhine more beautiful, though narrower. But after all, everyone to his taste!

From Prescott I crossed the river to see Ogdensburg, a small American city belonging to the State of New York. Then I left for Montreal. The country in general is sad-looking, poor and wretched. Certainly the season and the bad weather had a good deal to do with this. Most of the houses in the towns are good, with thatched roofs and they make a striking contrast with the churches built of stone and with tin roofs. The rapids of the St. Lawrence are worth seeing, and if I had not already shot a number of rapids, I should have gone down these in a canoe; but lack of time and especially the bad weather made me prefer the stage.

After going through various small towns and villages, which reminded me of the poorest and wretchedest villages of France, I reached Montreal. I went all over the city. There are many nice stone houses, very well-built, many and maybe too many churches and convents. The cathedral, which is consecrated to the Catholic faith, is the finest. It is newly built, and its architecture is in the Gothic style, very simple but very elegant. The French population is most religious; too religious, I venture to say, for the priests there have a huge influence, and having utterly forgotten that their reign ought not to be of this world, they poke their noses into everything, mix in politics, and naturally make common cause with the powerful and the aristocratic. I went into several bookstores where I found nothing but prayer-books and volumes on theology and other religious topics. There is a theatre at Montreal, but the priests are so strict that they forbid their charges to enter it; and the Protestant population is too small to support it alone.

I left in the evening on the "John Bull" for Quebec. The bad weather kept us from getting ahead. There I was 1/4 of the distance along, rocking at anchor, for the wind blew like the devil himself and a sort of frozen snow fell which cut your face. It was a torment such as I have experienced several times while crossing the Alps in the Winter. The vessel's deck was covered with ice, and it was only the 28 October. Blessed are the inhabitants of so mild a climate!

Finally I reached Quebec. The town and the sights it contains are nothing remarkable; but the view one gets from the ramparts of the citadel is incomparable. The bay formed by the St. Lawrence and the St. Charles, reminds one somewhat of the Bay of Naples. In America it is a general rule when one wishes to recommend some view, to say, "That's like the Bay of Naples. That's as fine as Italy." And though at times the comparison is as apt as if one compared a mushroom to a church tower, still it always infinitely flattered my national conceit.

But to return to the Quebec citadel, called Fort du Cap Diamant. In Europe this would be a fortress of the second class, but in North America, where there are neither fortresses nor armies to besiege them, it is a perfect Gibraltar, and even a little more.

The town of Quebec is divided into two: the lower town, built on the shore of the St. Lawrence, and the upper town, built on a rock and almost entirely surrounded by batteries. The monuments to Wolfe, Montcalm, Montgomery, amount to very little.

I visited the Parliament House, the Seminary, the Cathedral, which are not bad for a small town. I saw the marine hospital, and that certainly would not be out of place in a large city in Europe.

Quebec in general is rather dirty than clean, and not lighted at all, which gives rise to a great many murders; and I was assured that the Winter before, under a city gate where it is very dark, 16 people were killed, without the English police' having even taken the pains to put a lantern there, or a sentinel. The police in general, and here in particular, take too little interest in politics and too little in public safety. The soldier who acted as my guide for going over the fortifications, told me that the number of deserters was enormous, and that out of a regiment of 600 men which had arrived twelve days before, 16 had already run away. As the regiment had been moved to the citadel to prevent desertions, the last one who got away during the night, had taken the telegraph rope, which he had fastened to a gun-carriage and in that way had let himself down the face of the rock. I asked the soldier the reason for so much desertion, and he told me that you can earn more working in the United States, where you are not shut up in a fort and where the climate is less severe. Not so silly of them!

I visited the arsenal, which is like all the arsenals in the world: sabres and pistols are arranged in sun-bursts on the ceiling, and the muskets are stacked in piles. There were enough guns in the arsenal to fit out 50,000 men, and the keeper told me there were as many more inside the chests.

I went to see the Falls of Montmorency. Although they are 260 feet high, they make no impression after Niagara; not from the question of height, but because the mass of water is vastly less than at Niagara.

I returned to Montreal and remained there two days more. I took one morning to see the hill called Montreal from which the view over the St. Lawrence and the Ottawa is very pretty but not at all comparable to the panorama from Quebec.

I there became acquainted with a Mr. Papineau,* the O'Connell of Canada. It cannot be denied that he is a man who might shine in whatsoever circle, through his talent, his education, and above all his patriotism; but unfortunately I fear that he is illuding himself about the political convulsion that cannot long delay to make this unhappy country even worse. Canadians are courageous, very courageous when it is a question of risking their lives against ferocious wild animals or Indians; and I am sure that ten Canadians would dare defend themselves and not retreat one

*In 1837 French Canadians in Lower Canada, led by Louis Joseph Papineau, and some of the Upper Canadians under William Lyon Mackenzie, made an armed revolt against the governments of the two provinces. General Sir John Colborne, whom Arese mentions some lines later, quelled the revolt; and Papineau subsequently spent many years in banishment.

step against 60 Indians and even against a larger number; but on the other hand, I fear that ten red uniforms would put a hundred of those brave fellows to flight. It will be a matter simply of serving a hard apprenticeship, and after being conquered, they will, I hope, learn to conquer in their turn.

On board the steamboat I met General Colborne and his aide-de-camp, with whom I had a long talk; and they told me they had asked instructions from London and that meanwhile they would do nothing. I fear that when the confounded instructions come, they will be immediately followed by arrests, courts martial, and hangings.

One thing which, in my opinion, will put off the emancipation of this country, is the priests' influence. It is enormous, and I hardly need say that the altar upholds the throne, as the throne upholds the altar. Execrable reciprocity!

I happened to be at Montreal when the unsuccessful attempt at revolution broke out and I wrote to various friends in Europe what an unfortunate outcome I saw for it. The Liberals conspired publicly, and the revolt was announced beforehand by placards. If it were not that for political reasons it is valuable for England to keep

even in times long gone, forced us to sell our courage and our talents to foreigners. But our day will come. At least one must hope for it and hasten it with all one's might.

From Montreal I went to la Prairie (in a steamboat), and from there to St. John by rail. In the car where I was there were three Americans, who after talking of the weather, of the cold which was very bitter, started a political dissertation about Canada; and one of them said, "Oh, the French don't know how to fight. One American can make ten of them run." Although not French, I thought I ought to take that up, and after having told him that when the French came to fight for American independence, they had not run, and that maybe without their help America would still be an English colony, and other things equally forcible and unpleasant, I concluded my peroration by saying that I had a pair of pistols in my valise and should be enchanted to find out which one of us two would be the first to back. He hastened to excuse himself, he turned himself inside out and nearly killed himself with apologies and extenuations. I profited by the occasion to add that when one has the misfortune to be insolent, one should never be a coward.

At St. John I took the steamboat once more and

went up Lake Champlain to Whitehall. I think Lake Champlain must be magnificent in the good season, but unfortunately the Winter, then beginning, diminished its beauty a great deal. On board the steamboat were custom-house officials who to my great surprise, examined all our baggage thoroughly; and I believe that those at Dover or Calais could not be stricter; but to make up for that, they could easily be politer.

From Lake Champlain and from the road leading to Glenn's Falls and Saratoga there are fine views of the White Mountains and the Green Mountains. I wanted to go through both ranges and so to Boston, but the bad state of the roads made me decide to go straight to New York and from there to Boston by the East River. The country between Whitehall, Sandy Hill, Glenn's Falls, Saratoga, and Ballston is very lovely and most picturesquely cut up. All those places are fashionable and filled up in the Summer. At Glenn's Falls there is a cataract formed by the Hudson, which is a rather pretty river, though at Saratoga not very wide. At Ballston there are mineral springs, and there are immense bathing establishments building. The environs are magnificent.

From Saratoga, passing through Schenectady, I went by rail to Albany, the capital of the State of

New York. Albany is a very pretty town with fine buildings of stone and white marble. The Capitol, the City Hall, the Institute, the Academy, the Lyceum, several banks and handsome churches, are ornaments to the town. The traffic on the Hudson and the Erie Canal, and by railway, make this town quite lively.

From Albany I descended the Hudson to New York in a steamboat that made 18 miles an hour. Though I had already seen the beautiful North River, it was with new and lively pleasure that I now saw it once again, for its shores are as picturesque and lovely as heart could desire. After spending three or four days in New York to rest, I left by steamboat for Boston.

As far as Providence the East River, though much less beautiful than the Hudson, still does not fail to afford interesting views, and the pretty country houses that adorn its shores add much to the landscape. The penitentiary on Blackwell's Island is a huge mass of stone, and when seen from a certain distance gives quite the impression of a Mediæval castle.

I had visited that prison several months before. Well-organized though it is, it comes far from rivalling those in Philadelphia. Flushing Bay,*

* What is printed in the text is "Hoechin Bay." When Arese

Hellgate, and other points are worth a traveller's attention.

Providence is a small town on high ground, rather well-built; but I cannot say much about it, having seen it only while passing close by.

From Providence I left by railroad and after going through an insignificant region I reached Boston.

Boston is a handsome and a large town. Many people, especially Bostonians, find it the finest city in the United States. For my part, I prefer Philadelphia and even more New York. Boston much resembles an English town, and in its best quarters you might easily imagine you were in London. The panorama from the top of the City Hall (*sic*) is very beautiful.

Boston is built, so to speak, on an island, and united to the mainland around it only by six or eight bridges. It is called the Athens of America because its inhabitants are better educated than those of the other towns. The others revenge themselves by calling the Bostonians cold and stiff. As for me, I cannot judge, having stayed

instead of Fort McHenry wrote, I have no doubt, "Fort Henry," it was printed "Fort Fleury." This time I think the process of confusion between Fl and H was reversed. Very likely he wrote "Floechin," as an Italian well might on asking, "What is that over there?" and being told "Flushing."

there too short a time. The Dry Dock, a basin perfectly constructed of nothing but stone, serves for taking ships out of the water so as to re-cover them with copper. When I was there, they were covering the frigate "Ohio."

The Bostonians are proud of what they call their Père-la-Chaise, and dare to consider it on the same level and even higher than the one in Paris. "Blessed are the poor in spirit" says the Gospel. There is their epitaph all made for them! It is true that the situation of that cemetery is magnificent and that the view from the highest point is very extensive; but as for the monuments, the milestones on the post-roads in Italy would be admired here not merely for the granite they are made of, but also for their architectural good taste.

I went into several bookstores and found them well provided with foreign books, of which they had magnificent editions printed in Boston and able to bear comparison with the best English and French editions, and certainly superior to what is printed and engraved in the rest of Europe. But the rather high price of those works prevented me from supplying myself with as many as I should have liked.

I went through the Atheneum and the Museum which was built by public subscription. Among other things I noticed plaster casts of our best statues and groups, a collection of medals, and a pretty big library. The director, whose name I greatly regret having forgotten, a very nice man, showed me some precious manuscripts, and among the finest works one by my compatriot Giulio Ferrari.* If I mistake not, the title is *Costumes of All the Peoples in the World.* My national pride was so much excited by the lofty praises he sang of the works of Italy and the Italians, that I could not resist telling him that I belong to that beautiful and unhappy country. Then he added things most pleasant to a true patriot's ear, and informed me that Americans owe the best history of this country to an Italian, Carlo Botta.†

* Even in its Supplement the "Nuova enciclopedia italiana" does not mention Giulio Ferrari. But the fact is that either we have another misprint here or that Arese did not know his compatriot's name, which was Ferrario. The Boston Atheneum, in its latest catalogue lists it: "Ferrario, Giulio. Il costume antico e moderno; storia del governo, della milizia, relig., arti, ec. Milano, 1829. 18v. 4°."

† Of Botta's "Storia della guerra dell'indipendenza degli Stati Uniti d'America" (Paris, 1809, 4 vols.), Professor Edwin Erle Sparks says in Larned's "Literature of American History" (1902), "The most valuable of the earlier histories of the Revolution, and not yet considered antiquated. . . . The perspective of the history is bad in places, owing to its being based

I went to see the Market and other things of slight importance. I saw a tragedy very well acted in a fairly handsome theatre and before a better audience than is usually seen in New York. I went to see the University of Cambridge. I drove to Bunker Hill where the first battle was won against Great Britain's regular troops by simple American farmers, a victory that gave the Americans great confidence and served as overture to the great drama whose gigantic results we are now witnessing.

When Americans read in Fanny Kemble's travels of how a gentleman (if indeed he should be called that) seeing another on a steamboat brushing his teeth, asked him for the loan of his toothbrush when he was finished, and the other very kindly obliged him, but when the brush was returned threw it overboard: the first one was cross and wanted to know if the other thought he had a cleaner mouth than his (and perhaps he was thinking of the proverb that there's nothing cleaner than a dog's mouth) ; happily the matter was settled amicably—when, I say, Americans

on European sources. It follows classical forms in putting imaginary speeches into the mouths of the chief actors. A lofty style adds to the heroic mold in which the forefathers of the republic are cast."

read that little anecdote, they begin to yell, "What infamy! What a calumny!" And really it would seem to be a farcical accusation, a bad joke. But for my part I believe that the tale is, if not true, at least possible and even very probable, for at Boston the civilized town above all others, and at the Tremont House, the best and most fashionable hotel, there were in every room a nailbrush and a toothbrush for the use of all comers. Let us honor the truth!

After stopping three days in Boston, I returned by the same route to New York, where I stayed a month in order to pick up. Then I shipped for New Orleans. I visited Florida, Alabama, Louisiana, and from New Orleans I went to the West Indies. I saw the Spanish colonies of Havana. I went to Georgia, crossed South and North Carolina, and returned to New York after seven months' absence.

End of the TRAVEL NOTES

Postscript

BY THE TRANSLATOR

THE final proofs of this book had been read, when I learned from M. Henry Bordeaux's "Coeur de la Reine Hortense" (Paris, 1933) about Mlle. Masuyer's diary. Valérie Masuyer was "reader" to the Queen for seven years, taking part in the hegira from Italy, in the Strasbourg attempt, or rather in its results, and being present at the distressful death of her mistress, whom she sincerely loved. She seems also to have been somewhat in love with the Prince, and by her own confession, was decidedly so with Arese. Parts of her voluminous diary were published, at intervals during 1914-16, in the "Révue des deux mondes."

From it one learns that Arese probably did not, as one gathers from his biographer Bonfadini, hasten to Arenenberg with his offer of joining Louis Napoleon in New York, for the reason that he appears to have been at Arenenberg already.

From the report of one conversation of the Prince's,

after his return from New York, we discover that: "He talked to us about America, where mustaches are so much loathed that it is dangerous to wear one. From that he passed to his worrying about M. Arese, who has been so stubborn as not to be willing to shave his, and apropos of that he told us that he is very much in love (though he won't admit it) with an American, who is not pretty, but very rich and very likeable, whom the Prince strongly advised him to marry, — I must have turned pale, for my heart stopped, I felt as if I was going to faint. Can one imagine such silliness? It proved to me that, without knowing it, in spite of my good sense, he has played a more important rôle in my affections than I could have wished. I know quite well that he never felt love for me....The Prince showed us...a lot of views of New York. He repeated the news of M. Arese's love affair....

"The Prince added that M. Arese has taken such a distaste for Americans that it got on his nerves. One day when they were paying the Prince the honor of presenting to him, one after another, all the New York aldermen, M. Arese was so out of patience with the way it was done, that he kept saying to the Prince, 'If this doesn't stop, I will jump out the window,'—

and at everything the Prince said, he remarked, under his breath, 'But they don't understand you. These are pearls before swine.' He was right. Americans do not understand anything except business."

Some of Arese's letters are given; certain extracts from which may serve as a sort of prelude to his trip in the interior of America. On 3 April, 1837, he wrote from New York: "I am glad to tell you that the Prince has arrived at Norfolk, and in good health; in proof of which I send you the little gazette enclosed. . . . "

And on the 16 April: " . . . . Louis is well and is not unhappy. Yesterday we went to Long Island to see a little marine arsenal, and tomorrow we are going to visit the fortifications of the city of New York, and some of the environs. Balls, suppers, and dinners, and other gayeties are entirely suspended, because of the very bad state of business."

We all know of the depression of '37; but it may have been that Lent had something to do with the lack of entertainments.

"This last month there have been a hundred bankruptcies, for more than a hundred million francs, which results in the Prince's not having yet met the Society people of this town." Which might seem to uphold Hone, did we not know from other sources that the Prince was well acquainted with various excellent people, including Hone's great friend Washington Irving.

"We stay in the house a great deal and talk till our throats are dry. Yesterday evening the 'Columbus' packet from Liverpool arrived here, but because of Sunday we cannot have our mail till tomorrow morning, so that we shan't be able to answer it before the packet of the 24. I shall be very glad to start off, for I am fed up with New York."

Early in June he writes: " . . . . My friend leaves on Thursday, the 8, on board the 'George Washington,' and Heaven bless him and send him all the happiness he merits. If there had been any danger to fear, you may be sure I should not have deserted him; but as that is not the case, and as I can be of no use to him, I am going to stay in America, and in four days I am preparing to start on my perigrinations. I shall go to Philadelphia, Baltimore, Washington; across Virginia to see the mineral springs and the natural bridge; go down the Ohio to Cincinnati, Louisville; and up the Mississippi as far as Saint Louis. From there I am going up the Missouri as far as I can, and returning to Saint Louis to go on up the Mississippi. I will cross the Prairie du Chien, go to the falls of St. Anthony,

Fort Snelling, the River St. Pierre, and by way of the Lakes I shall return via Green Bay, Chicago, Detroit, Niagara, Montreal, Quebec, the St. Lawrence, and Boston, to New York. On the map it's a long distance, —between 5 or 6000 miles,—but you can travel so rapidly here that it is really nothing at all, and except one month when I shall go on horseback or on foot, all the rest will be by steamboat or stage. I am making this trip in poor company, my own; but it doesn't matter, I hope to find enough resources in myself to get along without other people. If Louis had come with me, I should not have cared about going so far; but being alone and not having to account to anybody for my existence, I will go just as far as I am able. . . . . "

It is remarkable how near he kept to his itinerary. The only change was in going across country to Fort Snelling (which in the diary appears as "For Cheltin") and down the Mississippi to Prairie du Chien, instead of retracing his Missouri voyage and going up the Mississippi from Saint Louis. The change was an improvement, since it gave him the most interesting part of his whole trip; although everything appears to have interested Arese.

A. E.

INDEX